STEPHANIE HOPPEN'S

DECORATING
WITH STYLE

STEPHANIE HOPPEN'S

DECORATING WITH STYLE

elegant details and creative solutions
for transforming your home

STEPHANIE HOPPEN

photographs by Violet Fraser

CLARKSON POTTER / PUBLISHERS

NEW YORK

To Julia, who helped make all this possible

Text copyright © Cico Books 2002
Photography by Violet Fraser © Cico Books 2002

Published by Clarkson Potter/Publishers, New York, New York.
Member of the Crown Publishing Group.
Random House, Inc. New York, Toronto, London, Sydney, Auckland
www.randomhouse.com

Clarkson N. Potter is a trademark and Potter and colophon are registered trademarks of Random House, Inc.
Originally published in Great Britain by Cico Books Ltd in 2002

Library of Congress Cataloging-in-Publication Data is available on request.
ISBN 0 609 61018 X
10 9 8 7 6 5 4 3 2 1
First American Edition

Text by Alexandra Parsons
Edited by Alison Wormleighton
Special photography by Violet Fraser
Designed by Michael Tighe

All photographs by Violet Fraser, © Cico Books, with the exception of:
© Jacques Dirand – page 10, 86
© Andreas von Einsiedel – page 10 (left), 15, 24 (bottom left), 27 (top right), 29 (top right), 120
© Andrew Wood – page 12 (top), 14, 16
© Inside Stock Image – The Interior Archive (Magazine: House and Leisure/C. Fraser) – 123
© Inside Stock Image – The Interior Archive (Magazine: Maison Francaise/P. von Robaeys) – 124, 128
© Inside Stock Image – The Interior Archive (Magazine: Deco Idees/S. Anton) – 144–145
page 42 - courtesy of Mark Brazier Jones
page 54, 95 - courtesy of Andrew Martin of Walton Street
page 140 (left and centre) - courtesy of Malcolm Martin
© Roy Fox/The Stephanie Hoppen Picture Archive; flat photography of artists' works throughout.

Printed and bound in Singapore

The author and publishers would like to thank the artists whose work is featured in photographs in this book:
Thierry Bosquet; Patrizia Medail; Maria Teresa Faini; Meg McCarthy; Mary Kuper; Thierry Flon; Lorioz; Yolanda Sonnabend; Michel Lablais; Antonella Casana; David Connell; Thierry Poncelet; Mariapia & Marinella Angelini. Flat photography of these works © Roy Fox/The Stephanie Hoppen Picture Archive.

CONTENTS

ACKNOWLEDGMENTS

Putting this book together has been a totally enjoyable and rewarding experience for me and I am scratching my head in a perplexed way as I try to think of how I can thank all my friends and colleagues who put in so much extra effort to get the results that I so badly wanted. Somehow just saying thank you does not seem enough for all those amazing and talented people who all went 'the extra mile'.

The team at Cico Books – we have now worked on three books together – a very rewarding experience for me.

Violet Fraser, my photographer, has been a delight to work with, and wherever we have worked together in the world she has never lost her cool or given up on me – she just keeps going till we get the right picture, no matter how late. And she always keeps her good humour.

Mike Tighe – a rare talent. His design of each page delights me in its unexpectedness and I have loved working with him as he seems to understand exactly what I want instantly – great for someone as impatient as I am.

Alex Parsons – my alter ego – my copious scribbled notes at the end of every shoot and my excited verbal comments are all polished, perfected, improved and gilded to make for a text that still sounds like me. Not an easy task.

To work with a team – Cindy, Violet, Mike and Alex – has been not only a delight but also a privilege. They are professional, talented, inspired and QUICK. I feel so lucky to have had this opportunity to collaborate with them on my book and I look forward to many future books together.

My friends, colleagues and family never seem to lose patience with me and continue to support me and provide me with all the wonderful homes I am allowed to photograph. They say a picture is worth a thousand words – I hope you will all agree with me that these photographs say it all.

To **Stuart Hands**, who is always by my side and helping, advising, rehanging and suggesting plus at the same time making delicious lunches for us all – thanks are not enough. Bless you, Stuart – you are a star. To David Cowdray, Stuart's partner, who never complains at the state of his home after we have worked there, a further thank you.

To **Anne Singer** my endless gratitude for her skill, talent, patience and good humour on the day before she moved house – this is friendship indeed.

It was a delight to work with **Julie Roil**, the Lanesborough Hotel florist, who gave us her unstinting help all day long and helped to make the seasonal tables so special.

To **Louise Bradley and her team,** my sincere thanks for all the time she gave to this project. Louise – my next door neighbour – always thinks up wonderful new ways of decorating spaces, and her style, generosity of spirit and practicality have been a joy.

To **Mr and Mrs Loay Al Naqib**, who gave us free rein in their exquisite home to photograph wherever we wanted, and who were helpful, hospitable and delightful no matter how long we stayed.

To **Colleen and Robert Bery** and the delightful **Bryony** – we had a wonderful day with you and you gave us a totally new dimension in trompe l'oeil. Your painted curtains, sisal carpets, cushions and walls will, I am sure, give all the readers endless ideas to change their homes with Quick Chic.

To **Anthony Stern and his team**, an enormous thank you for all their help at their busiest time – we have worked together on every book but you never make me feel bad about wanting to use your talent again and again.

To **Robbie Honey** for his inspired floral transformation of my kitchen – all of us who were there that day will always remember your mesmerizing work and your constant good humour.

To my darling **Rita Konig** who let me photograph her funky flat in London and cooked Violet and me a delicious lunch.

To **Danielle Moudabber**, for being allowed to photograph your amazingly stylish apartment – thank you. Your generosity in introducing me to so many talented artisans and artists is also much appreciated.

To **Kate Bannister** for once again allowing me to photograph her lovely home and disturb her cats.

To **Jessica Jessel** for her inspirational tables, that she created with enormous panache: thank you.

To **William Yeoward** and his wonderful team, for letting us photograph in Yeoward South, and then come back to re-photograph to get something absolutely right – a big thank you.

To **Chris Egerton** for getting my four-poster bed done in time for the photography and for his ability to read my mind and know exactly what I want.

To **Jennifer Brady** and **Helen Ballard Weeks** in Atlanta and to everyone in the Lake House and in the Atlanta home, an enormous thank you for your hospitality, generosity, constant enthusiasm and genuine friendliness – Violet and I will always remember our day at the Lake with great happiness.

Finally to **Julia Lowery**, to whom this book is dedicated – thank you for always being there, backing me up, finding things, reminding me, and making sure everything gets done. Thank you!

SHORT CUTS TO STYLE

INTERIORS SHOULD NEVER BE STATIC AND UNCHANGING. Moods change, lifestyles evolve and seasons bring their own magic. The kind of home I feel comfortable in is one that can go with the flow. This does not mean I am in favour of throwing out yesterday and buying a complete tomorrow – that would be both ridiculously expensive and wildly unsettling. It means slight shifts here and there with a repertoire of soft furnishings that disappear and reappear to great effect. It means having the courage to move things around to give them fresh impact. It is a state of mind that never thinks of a room as definitively 'finished', because to do so would fix you to the spot and leave no space for new enthusiasms.

It is amazing the effect a little courage has. Moving a picture from one side of the room to another can make all the difference between regarding the picture as visual wallpaper and actually seeing it again with fresh eyes. A change of curtains or blinds can dramatically alter the way light enters the room and also highlight or fudge an architectural feature. I love to play with throws and cushion covers, using creamy linens and crisp cottons for the cool looks of spring and summer, and then later on in the year, as winter draws in, replacing them with a snuggle of fake fur or big cosy cable knits.

In this book my aim is to show you how to use style as a quick fix without having to resort to complete redecoration. As well as my own apartment, the book shows many inspired decorative touches I've found in the homes of some very creative people who have been generous enough to let us photograph there. You will find ingenious ways to make a room lighter and brighter or warmer and cosier, and get some spectacular ideas for 'dressing' a room for a special occasion. This is a particular passion of mine as I love the idea of using a home as a theatrical set for staging weddings, Christmases and other special occasions. You will see also how rehanging pictures and rearranging collections can alter the mood of a room completely, and discover the massive impact that seasonal flowers and beautiful table settings can have on any interior.

Stephanie Hoppen

1

TRANSFORMATIONS
Case studies
in metamorphosis

WHEN FAMILIARITY STARTS TO BREED dissatisfaction, it's time to rethink and revamp, to stage a subtle change of emphasis that redirects the eye and brings a tired look up to date and beyond. In this chapter I have put together some 'before and after' sequences, many of them in my own apartment, in order to prove my own theory. Given that I have very little free time to devote to decorating my own home, I think I have proved that transformations can be achieved in no time at all – it's the art of the subtle shift.

Basically, the transformations in this chapter are not about calling in the builders and suffering weeks of disruption and huge bills, or wrestling with dustsheets, paintbrushes and wallpaper paste. These are transformations brought about by looking around at what you have before you look elsewhere, and moving things around a bit to give a fresh perspective on your possessions. It is amazing the difference you can make just by changing a curtain or a light fitting, or buying a new tablecloth or a new set of bedlinen.

MY ENTRANCE HALL doubles as a dining room and is designed to be dramatic. Warm and welcoming, it twinkles with light from a chandelier and myriad mirrors. It has no natural light source – no window or skylight – so I used as many mirrors as I could, even down to mirrored picture frames, but it still wasn't quite enough. Then Nina Campbell came up with the idea of lining the back of my cabinet with mirror glass, giving me sparkle on all four walls. Brilliant!

I love the general feel of the room and wouldn't want to touch the red hand-painted walls or the witty pictures, but I felt it was getting a little cluttered. I have a lovely tapestry cloth that has graced my circular table for six years and I usually ring seasonal changes with flower arrangements. The 'before' shots show two different tall flower arrangements and sparkling glass accessories, but a real transformation requires more than just a change of flowers.

I asked Colleen Bery (see page 36) to make me a raspberry-coloured silk cloth to throw over the tapestry and some new terracotta-coloured curtains to replace the heavy red chenille. I now had a rich and interesting collection of warm hues in my hall including shades of raspberry and terracotta, which all blended beautifully and instantly made the room seem lighter, brighter and a great deal larger. I then decided to clear the table of all the bits and pieces that had accumulated over the years and dream up a whole new tablescape. Anthony Stern, a talented glass blower, loaned me nine of his magnificent tall latticinio bottles of varying heights, and the effect was instantly dramatic. The tall, linear shapes are modern and uncluttered but they have that opulent old Venetian look that I love.

above THREE RECENT TRANSFORMATIONS TO MY HALL TABLE,
WHICH RETAINED ITS WELCOMING WARMTH WHILE ENJOYING AN
UPDATE. THE MAJOR CHANGE WAS THE RASPBERRY CLOTH.
left THE GROUP OF ANTHONY STERN LATTICINIO BOTTLES GAVE
THE ROOM AN INSTANT DOSE OF MODERNITY. I ADDED THE HIGH-
BACKED CHAIR TO EMPHASIZE THE VERTICAL SHAPES.

above TWO VIEWS OF MY FAVOURITE ANTHONY STERN PIECE, A
HUGE GLASS BOWL. IN THE TOP PICTURE IT HAS BEEN FILLED
WITH WHITECURRANTS FOR DINNER-PARTY GUESTS TO PICK AT,
AND IN THE LOWER PICTURE IT IS FILLED WITH FLAT WHITE
SHELLS THAT ARE THERE SIMPLY TO BE ADMIRED.
right MY BLUE AND WHITE KITCHEN TRANSFORMED INTO A RICH
AND RARE OLD MASTER PAINTING. AN ADDED PAINTERLY TOUCH
IS THE TROMPE L'OEIL SUNHAT 'HANGING' ON THE DOOR

MY KITCHEN IS BASICALLY BLUE AND WHITE, and it has provided the backdrop for many memorable parties. Usually I play up the blue and white theme, often leaving the wooden table bare, but the occasion of a small family wedding breakfast gave me the excuse to go for an opulent autumn transformation (see pages 12–13). I made the walls look richer, not by painting them a warmer colour but by swapping the pictures around, concentrating on paintings in gilded or trompe l'oeil tortoiseshell frames. Colleen Bery found me a painted cloth in earthy shades of terracotta that swept dramatically to the floor. She then painted a silk strip with an overall design to run down the centre of the table, finishing it off with gilded tassels.

The inspirational florist Robbie Honey created a breathtaking cascade of autumn flowers as the centrepiece for my table, which now looked as if it belonged in the banqueting hall of an Italian count. He filled a giant goblet made by Anthony Stern with floral foam and built up a framework of large green leaves. He then built the cascade with large dried hydrangeas, pomegranate halves stuck on bamboo poles, three shades of cream roses, millet (Milium), snowberries and foliage. The leftover pomegranates were piled into a favourite silver swan. This cornucopia of fruits, flowers and trailing leaves, combined with mother-of-pearl plates and softly gleaming silver, turned my blue and white kitchen into a glowing Old Master painting. The effect was magical.

left MY KITCHEN LOOKING WHITE AND COOL. THE WOODEN TABLE IS SET WITH WHITE CHINA, SILVER AND GLASS, AND TWO SAUCEBOATS ARE FILLED WITH WHITE ANEMONES. I'VE PUT WHITE SHELLS AND FLOWERS ON THE SHELVES AND MOVED THE PICTURES AROUND AGAIN, FAVOURING ONES WITH WHITE GROUNDS.

below THIS TIME I HAVE EMPHASIZED THE BLUE WITH BLUE FLOWERS, BLUE CHINA AND ANOTHER SHUFFLE OF THE PICTURES AND OBJETS ON THE SHELVES. I'VE HAD THE CHAIRS FOR 15 YEARS. THE SEATS ARE UPHOLSTERED IN A BLUE FORTUNY FABRIC, BUT WHEN I WHIP THEM THROUGH TO MY RED DINING ROOM, I TRANSFORM THEM WITH TIE-ON COVERS IN A LOVELY RED INDIAN PAISLEY FABRIC.

left: LOUISE BRADLEY'S COOL WHITE SITTING ROOM DRESSED FOR SUMMER. VENETIAN-STYLE MIRRORS ARE VERY POPULAR NOW – I LOVE THEM BECAUSE THEY ARE DRAMATIC AND LOOK GREAT IN MODERN AND PERIOD SETTINGS.
opposite: THE SITTING ROOM DRESSED FOR WINTER. A CHANGE OF ACCESSORIES AND A LOVELY RED VELVET CHAIR GIVE THE ROOM A WARM GLOW.

A SEASONAL TRANSFORMATION has turned designer Louise Bradley's lovely icy white sitting room into a cosy winter retreat. She replaced the urns of white flowers and trailing ivy with neat green topiary in smart tin boxes. The candlesticks went, as did the stone lion in the corner, to make way for larger pieces of furniture. The curvy white footstool in front of the fire was put away and two leopardskin footstools were moved in along with a red velvet chair with tapestry cushions.

The soft, rich textures of velvet and fur are perfect for the warm winter look. The walls, of course, have remained the same colour, a lovely rich parchment contrasted with white woodwork and a white ceiling. What is so clever about this transformation, which took no time at all to achieve, is that the walls, which looked so cool and calm in the summer version, took on a much warmer hue thanks to the proliferation of texture and the splashes of colour.

Seasonal changes can be achieved in moments with cushions and throws, and this is why I am so fond of using them. You pack up your soft linens and crisp cottons as autumn approaches and dig out something warm and cosy, adding a dash of jewel-like colour, and the room glows. Flowers, of course, are instant seasonal fixes – daffodils and tulips say spring as clearly as roses say summer. Apart from using seasonal flowers and foliage to speak for me, I like to change the vases too, using clear glass and white containers in the summer to emphasize the freshness of the greenery, and substituting coloured glass and earthy-toned ceramics during the winter months.

I WANTED TO SHOW HOW A BEDROOM could change character dramatically without any major remedial work, by using different bedlinen and accessories. I asked Anne Singer of London's Monogrammed Linen Shop to help me, even though she was about to move house and was staying in a friend's rented apartment. The bedroom of this apartment, shown on pages 20–23, has a stunning antique Japanese screen as a bedhead, which gives the room a calm linear quality.

For the winter bedroom Anne chose fine linen sheets with the very palest blush of pink and a cashmere blanket that matched the sheets exactly. Instead of covering the bed in an all-encompassing quilt, Anne added a surprise in the form of a faux-fur zebra-print throw, which echoed the black and white of the framed photographs and looked great against the backdrop of the Japanese screen. The pale pink flowers in the vase on the bedside table also match the blush pink of the sheets. They are old-fashioned country roses with a delicious scent.

The summer transformation was achieved using blue and white, zebra-patterned Porthault sheets and pillowcases. This is a very old Porthault design, recoloured by Anne and printed exclusively for the Monogrammed Linen Shop. Again the design on the bedlinen works well with the Japanese screen, and the blue cashmere blanket folded across the end of the bed matches the blue in the sheets exactly. The crisp white bedcover in classic French cotton piqué adds to the summery feel. The oriental bedside tables echo the Japanese theme, as do the ancient ivory objects and the finely woven baskets. The torpedo-shaped lamp standing on the floor is woven too; it is a beautiful object in itself and an exciting way of combining illumination with sculpture.

THE TRANSFORMATION OF MY OWN BEDROOM is a saga in its own right. In its first guise (see page 24, bottom left photograph), the bedhead was made to incorporate a lovely carved wooden overdoor garland that I couldn't resist during a visit to an antiques shop in the South of France. I had chosen pictures of elegant ladies in lovely dresses in their original gilded frames, and my hand-embroidered curtains were a graceful sweep of blue and white, lined with gingham and tied back low down to make the most of the lovely proportions of the French doors that open onto my balcony (see page 27).

right: A PERFECT EXAMPLE OF A QUICK FIX, PHOTOGRAPHED IN THE ATLANTA HOME OF HELEN BALLARD WEEKS. ELEGANT WHITE DINING ROOM CHAIRS UPHOLSTERED IN AN EMBOSSED PIERRE FREY FABRIC UNDERGO A TRANSFORMATION FOR FAMILY MEALS. THE SIMPLE SLIPCOVERS ARE OF PRINTED COTTON. opposite: LOUISE BRADLEY'S DOG MARNI, POSING LIKE THE TRUE STARLET SHE IS, IN THE RED VELVET CHAIR – THE KEY PIECE IN LOUISE'S WINTER MAKEOVER.

ANNE SINGER'S BEDROOM IN ITS WINTER MODE,
WITH SHEETS OF THE PALEST PINK AND A CASUAL SPRAWL
OF PILLOWS. THIS BEDROOM IS BRILLIANTLY ACCESSORIZED.
ANIMAL PRINTS AND FRAMED BLACK AND WHITE
PHOTOGRAPHS ARE VERY STRONG TRENDS, AND ONES I
REALLY LIKE. THE TWO ELEMENTS WORK WELL TOGETHER,
BEING SIMULTANEOUSLY ENIGMATIC AND DRAMATIC.

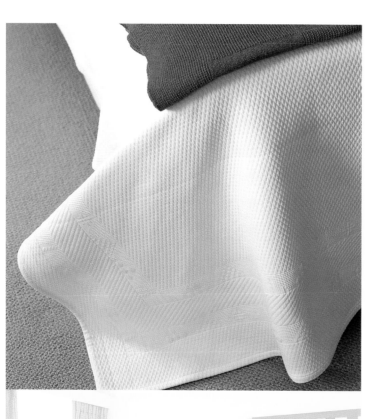

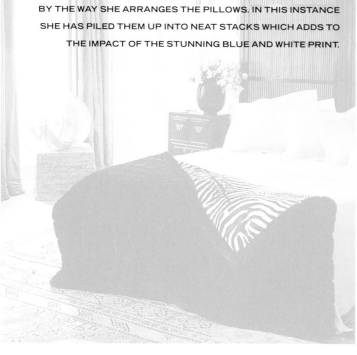

above A DETAIL OF THE THICK, WHITE FRENCH COTTON PIQUÉ
BEDCOVER IN ANNE SINGER'S SUMMERTIME BEDROOM.
right ANNE'S BEDROOM HAS A DIFFERENT ATMOSPHERE NOW.
IT'S CRISP AND BLUE AND THAT IS LARGELY DUE TO THE WAY
THE BED HAS BEEN MADE UP. I LEARNED SO MUCH WORKING
WITH ANNE: SHE CAN ALTER THE FEEL OF A BEDROOM JUST
BY THE WAY SHE ARRANGES THE PILLOWS. IN THIS INSTANCE
SHE HAS PILED THEM UP INTO NEAT STACKS WHICH ADDS TO
THE IMPACT OF THE STUNNING BLUE AND WHITE PRINT.

right MY NEW VENETIAN FOUR-POSTER LOOKING NEAT AND
TAILORED WITH A VELVET AND CASHMERE BEDCOVER.
far right THE SAME ROOM WITH A MORE ABANDONED LOOK,
ACHIEVED WITH A MASS OF PILLOWS AND A FAUX FUR THROW.
below MY BEDROOM BEFORE THE TRANSFORMATION. I HAD
CHOSEN AN OLD-FASHIONED ANTIQUE LACE AND
EMBROIDERY LOOK WHICH SUITED THE ELABORATELY
CARVED HEADBOARD.
below right ANOTHER BEDROOM IN MY HOME, WITH A BED BY
LOUISE BRADLEY. THE SMOKY GREY-BLUE WALLS SUIT THE
BED AND THE CHEEKY LORIOZ PAINTINGS PERFECTLY.

I felt it was time for a change, and I wanted a faded eighteenth-century Venetian look. I had been searching for a four-poster bed for a very long time, but I could never find what I wanted. I didn't want one with fabric everywhere because I was not after a heavy look. Besides, I am allergic to all sorts of things and didn't want to be hemmed in by yards of dusty fabric. In the end I got together with Chris Egerton, a talented designer and maker of picture frames and furniture, and we decided that the only option was to make four poles to go at each corner of the bed. We worked on the style, inspired by the gondoliers' mooring poles on Venice's Grand Canal. Chris had the poles made and then got down to the lengthy business of giving them that distressed look I'm so fond of. The four posts have totally transformed the room. They are bolted to the floorboards rather than to the frame, so the bed is easy to make. The look is so successful that Chris and I are thinking of going into production.

As always, I asked Anne Singer of the Monogrammed Linen Shop to dress the bed. My brief was for a simple, tailored look in linen, and she did this beautifully. In fact, she produced two looks for me, one crisp and unfussy with the pillows neatly piled and a velvet and cashmere tweed bedcover, and the other more abandoned, with lots of upended pillows, a luxurious cashmere blanket and a faux tigerskin throw.

top MY BEDROOM WINDOW BEFORE THE TRANSFORMATION.
above THE WONDERFUL ORGANZA AND PASHMINA CURTAINS,
MADE FOR ME BY STUART HANDS, IN THEIR FIRST PHASE.
left THE CURTAINS NOW HAVE A LITTLE ORGANZA PELMET
WHICH SOFTENS THE TOP AND A GAUZY BLIND THAT IS
BARELY THERE YET GIVES ME PRIVACY. THE CUPBOARD ON
THE FAR LEFT CONTAINS A TV AND VCR, AND ON TOP OF IT,
FILLED WITH SILK FLOWERS, I KEEP MY FAVOURITE ANTHONY
STERN BOWL WHEN IT IS NOT WANTED IN THE DINING ROOM.

above right THE BAY WINDOW IN MY SITTING ROOM USED TO HAVE
A ROUND TABLE WITH A FLOOR-LENGTH SILK CLOTH.
above I MOVED THE ROUND TABLE TO THE OTHER SIDE OF THE
ROOM. HERE IT HAS BEEN LAID FOR AN INTIMATE DINNER.
left NOW MY BAY WINDOW LOOKS MUCH MORE OPEN AND LIGHT AND
PROVIDES A GREAT PLACE TO KEEP MY CANDLESTICK COLLECTION.

Two years ago, I tackled the curtains at the bay window in my bedroom (see pages 26–27). I wanted something flowing and soft, simple yet luxurious. I started with the pelmet, which was made from a pair of antique gilt wood pelmets skilfully crafted into one pelmet by Antonio Scialo, a talented gilder. The curtains are layers of pashmina and silk organza and were made by Stuart Hands. They are totally wonderful, airy and light. But recently I got tired of always having to close the curtains, as I had no blind. My blue and white arrangement incorporated a roller blind, but I didn't want to block out the glow of light in that way again. I asked Colleen Bery to paint the faintest white-on-white design on a piece of organza, and she and Stuart made a blind out of it. The result is amazing. If you look at the window you get only the barest idea that there's something between you and the glass, yet from the outside looking in, the window is obscured. They also made a tiny organza pelmet to go under the gilded one, which softened the top edge of the curtains. The blue and white stool that had stood at the end of my bed for five years I reupholstered in a smart cream herringbone, and this sits in the bay draped in the faux fur throw (shown on page 83) when the throw is not needed on the bed. The window seems almost twice as big as it did before, and the light filters through the soft whites, warming up even the greyest of days.

THE BAY WINDOW IN MY SITTING ROOM is the first thing you see when you enter the room. I used to have the area in front of the window set up as a place to sit and chat, with upholstered chairs and a round table covered in a floor-length cloth. I now have a rectangular Majorcan table with a lovely, sculptural base, and on it I have grouped my collection of glass candlesticks interspersed with glass single-stem vases. It looks so much lighter and brighter now. If you achieve a pleasing look in a room, I know that it's very tempting to leave it there, year in year out, but it really limits the amount and variety of objects you can display and enjoy. I like to store things out of sight for a while and surprise myself by swapping them around. Absence may not make the heart grow fonder but it certainly sharpens up the eye.

STYLING SECRETS

Witty juxtapositions, fabulous faux paint
finishes, a sparkle of mirror and glass
and a wealth of stimulating ideas

THERE IS A WAY OF PUTTING A ROOM TOGETHER with bits from here and there and ideas you've picked up from who knows where, and it all adds up to serendipity. It's not a question of 'oh, if we had the money…' because you can cram a room with the most expensive items money can buy and it can still look like a furniture showroom. In this section of the book I've grouped together interiors that have been put together with bravura and flair – rooms full of inspired decorative touches to banish any fixed ideas of what goes with what. The owners of these rooms have often broken the 'rules' to create interiors that truly reflect their personalities, because that's what a home should be: a showcase for you, your personal statement, not a safe, inoffensive space that won't frighten the neighbours.

DANIELLE MOUDABBER came to study art history in London via Nigeria and the Lebanon, which may, in part, explain the funky, eclectic and dramatic flair displayed in her surroundings. She has created this memorable apartment from what used to be a 40-foot (12-metre) ballroom on the first floor of a London redbrick house. Her unique style, based on Art Deco

above and above right PERIOD PIECE TURNED FUNKY: THE ORIGINAL VICTORIAN PLASTERWORK IN DANIELLE'S HOUSE, PICKED OUT WITH SILVER PAINT.
above centre AN ETHEREAL STATUETTE OF DANIELLE BY CATY BURKEMAN AND A LAMP BY MARK BRAZIER-JONES.
opposite DANIELLE'S DINING AREA. ON THE TABLE ARE EXAMPLES OF DANIELLE'S WORK IN SHAGREEN, A MATERIAL MADE FROM THE SKIN OF THE STINGRAY.

antiques, ethnic art and the work of a host of talented young designers, gains inspiration from everywhere she goes. Danielle designs and makes a deluxe range of shagreen and leather handbags and home accessories.

Danielle's home is an object lesson in styling. Everything she puts together really works. Focusing on the bare bones of her high-ceilinged and panelled living room, she has played up the proportions of the room, retained the original parquet flooring and painted the fireplace, overmantel and chandelier with silver and aluminium, turning them into works of art in their own right. She has used furniture sparsely and has left the tall windows uncluttered by curtains so the eye is drawn towards the beautiful and surprising objects and paintings that make the room so uniquely hers. In her playful way, Danielle has continued the silver theme throughout the house. The original ceiling mouldings and baseboards together with the walls in her comparatively small bedroom have been painted silver, and the result is a feeling of modern opulence in the unashamedly Victorian room.

The dining end of the living room features an original rosewood table and chairs designed by Jacques Adnet and dating from 1939. She has flanked the strong modern paintings with 1940s vases, placed a cream and green ceramic piece so it picks up the hues from the painting and commissioned Mark Brazier-Jones to make delicate but eccentric-looking wall lights from nickel and glass. And there she has stopped. Much of the art of styling lies in knowing where to stop.

A VIEW OF DANIELLE'S SITTING AREA. THE CHANDELIER IS ANOTHER PERIOD PIECE THAT DANIELLE BROUGHT UP TO DATE WITH A TOUCH OF SILVER PAINT.

THE HOME OF COLLEEN AND ROBERT BERY is an absolute feast for the senses. There's pattern on pattern, texture on texture, and all in the rich and faded colours you would expect to find in an old Venetian palazzo. But the elaborate embroidery and fabulous woven patterns that you see on the carpets are fake. They are all hand-painted. The Berys were both art teachers, spending their evenings and weekends painting every scrap of wall and fabric in their home until it looked like a French chateau. Now they have been persuaded to make hand-painted fabrics and rugs their business, and their home has become a temple to this fabulous look.

Hand-painting the way the Berys do it is neither quick nor easy; it requires an enormous amount of skill. Their characteristic shading techniques, for instance, are achieved using artist's brushes and a minimum of eight specially mixed colours and gold pigments. They paint on every weight of fabric, from silk organza to velvet, and the rug designs are painted onto hard-wearing sisal. The stunning living room curtains are made of lined and interlined silk. The outer curtains are painted in subtle shades of pink and green, and the lining material, which has been cleverly rolled and folded over so you can see it, is a seriously deep pink. Pink is a great colour at a window because the light that shines through it is suffused with a warm, sunny glow.

If you are feeling artistic, you could take inspiration from these pages and try your hand at doing it yourself. I would recommend starting on artist's canvas, which is cheap enough to throw away if you make a botch of it, and comes in all kinds of weights, from muslin to heavy-duty sailcloth. It is used a lot by set designers and so it comes by the yard (meter) in conveniently wide widths and can be bought from artist's supply shops. The secret to styling this lovely, opulent, overblown look is to concentrate on mixing the patterns and then throw in something surprising, like the Berys have done with the touches of leopardskin among all those classical scrolls and borders. This way the room becomes a celebration of going over the top rather than a conventional attempt at grandeur. They have not stinted on fringing, swagging and fancy pelmets, and the Empire-style furniture is all of a piece, yet the walls are a calm shade of yellow and decorative objects are kept to a minimum. A simple bouquet of spring flowers is displayed in nothing grander than a white jug.

THE RUG IN THE BERY LIVING ROOM IS 25 YEARS OLD, HAS BEEN SUBJECTED TO ENDLESS WEAR AND TEAR FROM CHILDREN AND DOGS AND STILL LOOKS AMAZING. IT RESEMBLES A FADED ANTIQUE AUBUSSON CARPET THAT WOULD COST THE EARTH.

above left A CREAM-FRINGED THROW PAINTED TO
RESEMBLE CREWELWORK.

above THE CURVY CHAISE IS UPHOLSTERED IN PAINTED
SILK. ONLY THE BRAIDS AND TASSELS ARE FOR REAL.

left A DETAIL OF THE SETTEE IN THE BERYS' LIVING ROOM
SHOWING A PAINTED VELVET CUSHION ON PAINTED
SILK UPHOLSTERY.

above right A CHUNKY GILDED ROUNDEL HOLDS BACK
A CURTAIN PAINTED WITH THE *FOUGERE* DESIGN.

above far right VERY VERSAILLES – A BEADED TIEBACK
ADDS SPARKLE TO AN *EMPIRE TRELLIS* CURTAIN.

right THE CURTAINS IN THE BERYS' LIVING ROOM ARE MADE
OF LAYERS OF FABRIC IN GLORIOUS SHADES OF PINK.

far right A DETAIL OF THE PAINTED LEOPARDSKIN THAT
ADDS A TOUCH OF WIT TO THE PATTERN-ON-PATTERN LOOK.

THE BERYS' INVITING LIVING ROOM WHERE ENDLESS PATTERNS SIT HAPPILY TOGETHER. IT ALL LOOKS VERY GLAMOROUS, BUT IT'S HARD-WEARING TOO, AND OSCAR THE DOG IS NOT BANNED FROM SITTING ON THE UPHOLSTERY. COLLEEN HAS PAINTED AN EGYPTIAN-STYLE FRIEZE AT CORNICE HEIGHT, TO ADD YET ANOTHER PATTERN TO THE DELICIOUSLY ECCENTRIC MIX.

ECCENTRIC ACCENTS are what define a style as your own. While I would never urge anyone to copy someone else's style to the letter, there's nothing wrong with drawing heavily upon the inspiration. On these pages you can see some wild touches of leopardskin, all of it fake, of course, as real skins are a bit of a challenge to the ecologically aware. Fake fur is wonderful stuff, too, and I find that little touches of it here and there – in the form of a bedspread, a throw or a cushion – give out good signals. Fur equates with warmth and luxury, and what better ambience could you hope to create for your family and friends? A leopardskin-patterned stair carpet leads up to the bedroom floor in the Atlanta townhouse of Helen Ballard Weeks. (You can see other pictures of this amazing house on pages 18 and 93.) I like the way she has accented the brown and cream of the skin with the paintwork on the treads and risers.

On the subject of leopardskin, I find the towels scattered around one of the bathrooms of the Al Naqibs' London house totally seductive. (See more of the house on pages 45–49 and page 88.) They give the room a strong, masculine, 'Out of India' feel that is reinforced by the wooden blinds and the turned wood screen, with its subtle oriental look.

Occasional chairs can always be used to ring the changes and create a bit of a flutter. The great thing is that they are one-offs that don't have to 'fit' into the rest of the scheme. You can have one Le Corbusier lounger, one Rietveld chair or any other of the design classics and no one will expect you to have two. And you can move them around from room to room so they never lose their impact. The basket-weave bedroom chair in the Ballard Weeks house, pictured opposite, gets its stunning and memorable look from the leopardskin cushions. Mark Brazier-Jones's zebra-patterned chair, shown here, is also impossible to ignore – it looks as if it were alive and would follow you to the ends of the earth. It automatically makes people smile and want to stroke it. I visualize it in a dark red hallway, stunningly lit, or as the only colour accent in an otherwise all-white room. Either way I want one!

left MARK BRAZIER-JONES'S AMAZING CHAIR IS CRAFTED FROM ALUMINIUM AND CALFSKIN PRINTED WITH A ZEBRA PATTERN. right and above far right TWO VIEWS OF ZEIN AL NAQIB'S SECOND BATHROOM SHOWING THE IMPACT OF HER WONDERFUL LEOPARDSKIN TOWELS. far right and above right EXOTIC AND STYLISH TOUCHES OF LEOPARDSKIN IN THE ATLANTA HOME OF HELEN BALLARD WEEKS.

far left ZEIN AL NAQIB'S TEXTURAL ARRANGEMENT OF DRIED ARTICHOKES IN A DECORATIVE IRON URN.

left ANNIE KHAN'S CLEVER DOUBLE ARRANGEMENT. THE HYDRANGEAS AND ROSES WERE PLACED IN A SEPARATE GLASS VASE FITTED INSIDE THE LARGER ONE.

below far left ZEIN'S OVERBLOWN PEONIES. I LIKE THE WAY SHE HAS USED A FEW JUGS OF THEM ON THE TABLE.

below left ARTICHOKES ARE A FAVOURITE WITH LOUISE BRADLEY TOO.

this page THIS WINDOW IN ZEIN'S LONDON HOME WITH ITS LITTLE STAINED GLASS INSETS IS FAR TOO PRETTY TO COVER UP WITH CURTAINS. ZEIN HAS PLACED IN FRONT OF IT A LOVELY COLLECTION OF OBELISKS AND OTHER ZEN-LIKE OBJECTS, CHOOSING ELONGATED BRANCH-LIKE SHAPES TO EMPHASIZE THE FINE TRACERY OF THE LEADWORK ON THE WINDOW.

left DETAIL OF THE FRENCH IRONWORK CONSOLE TABLE
THAT LOUISE BRADLEY FOUND FOR HER OWN HOME.
right THIS FABULOUS PAIR OF ANTIQUE FRENCH GLAZED
DOORS WITH IRONWORK INSETS IN ZEIN'S HOUSE
WAS ORIGINALLY SPOTTED BY LOUISE IN AN
ARCHITECTURAL SALVAGE YARD.

THINKING LATERALLY ABOUT FLOWERS can produce some striking arrangements, as the examples on pages 44–45 show. Artichoke heads can be as beautiful as any flower, and in one case Louise has simply piled them into a big glass vase. Zein Al Naqib has made them look very formal, stacking them in a careful pyramid in an iron urn, and she has epitomized summertime with an abundance of overblown peonies in pretty little containers. Annie Khan has created a distinctly autumnal feel, with ornamental cabbages piled at the bottom of a glass vase and dried hydrangeas massed at the top.

LOUISE BRADLEY IS AN INTERIOR DESIGNER with a great sense of style. Not only does she create wonderful homes for her clients in London and abroad, with painstaking attention to detail, but she also has two shops selling the gorgeous things she picks up all over the world, as well as designs she has made exclusively for her shops. Louise has recently come up with a new and exciting direction, and we feature in this book a number of rooms designed by her. The examples shown here and on the next few pages illustrate Louise's eye for styling and her knack for creating surprise and delight.

The library window in Zein Al Naqib's house (pictured on pages 45 and 82) has its original nineteenth-century leading pattern, and it would be a shame to cover it up with curtains or blinds. A good solution for a pretty window is to

above, above right and right THIS MASCULINE APARTMENT
DESIGNED BY LOUISE BRADLEY TAKES LEATHER, HORN AND
LACQUER AS ITS INSPIRATION. SHE HAS ADDED SPARKLING
HIGHLIGHTS WITH DECORATIVE GLASS. I LIKE THE WAY SHE HAS
HUNG AN ORNATE VENETIAN MIRROR ON SOLID CHAINS.

semi-obscure the views to passers-by with a floral arrangement on the inside. In front of that window, a wide table has been covered in plants and books, so it has a random feel to it. The plant in the goblet-shaped urn is an unusual houseplant – it's a magnolia tree.

Wrought iron is very much part of Louise Bradley's lexicon. She sourced an amazing base for a console table (see page 46) and then went on the hunt for decorative banisters, candelabra and standard lamp bases. Because wrought iron makes a very bold decorative statement, you don't need much of it, and of course it brings a period feel with it unless you can persuade an ironwork studio to make up something to a modern design. A good place to look for wrought iron pieces is in architectural salvage yards. You can then have them cleaned up and turned into the piece of furniture or architectural feature you want, be it a table or a pair of doors.

Louise created a distinctive look in the apartment pictured here. The walls are covered in brown leather, and large mirrors give an illusion of spaciousness. The room shown above looks masculine and ordered, with the clean lines of the sofa and lacquered coffee table, but it gets a unique twist thanks to the ornate iron chandelier and an edge of comfort and colour from a fur throw and a champagne cooler filled with bud roses. The decorative objects chosen for the coffee table are as unique as the surroundings: a silver-rimmed horn drinking chalice to echo the horn wall sconces, and a pair of ostrich-skin vases.

above THE DESIGNER RITA KONIG PICKED UP A BARGAIN IN THIS 1950S ILLUMINATED MIRROR. NOW IT LENDS ITS CONSIDERABLE PERIOD CHARM TO A MODERN BATHROOM. right THE MAIN BATHROOM IN ZEIN AL NAQIB'S HOME. THE MAGNIFICENT BATH IS A RARE PIECE OF ARCHITECTURAL SALVAGE, AND LOUISE BRADLEY DESIGNED THE BATHROOM TO SHOW IT OFF. NOW IT SITS SURROUNDED BY MOSAIC AND LIT WITH VENETIAN GLASS SCONCES.

It is not the ostrich skin one usually sees, but the skin from the legs, which has more texture and looks more like baby crocodile skin. The study (shown on page 49) in the same apartment has the leather walls, the strong masculine furniture and the shock contrast factor, in this case the Venetian glass mirror. Vellum books, horn inkwells and a massive ammonite on a marble stand complete the look.

The main bathroom of Zein Al Naqib's apartment (see pages 50–51) makes use of Venetian mirrors behind wall sconces and basins. The bathroom looks spacious and airy, as if it has been flooded with Italian sunlight. To keep the sybaritic marble theme going, Louise found a stucco plaque of gambolling puttis and installed a mosaic floor. The lighting is soft and the surfaces uncluttered, resulting in a bathroom that is as stunning to look at as it is practical to use.

THE LAKESIDE HOME OF HELEN BALLARD WEEKS near Tallulah Falls, Georgia, pictured here and on the remaining pages of this chapter, is stylishly rustic and easy to live in. Looking like a log cabin from the outside, it fits snuggly into the landscape, and from the inside, large windows invite the lake views to be part of the home. The seductive palette of brown, cream and soft green imparts harmony, tranquillity and peace, reminiscent of lazy holidays in the warm South. The rooms lead effortlessly one into another, children skitter past, dogs find comfortable spots to curl up in and there are racks of coats, shoes and umbrellas just where you need them. Doorstops are made from large stones with rings set into them. Curtains are barely there – soft, understated afterthoughts in the simplest of fabrics. Ferns are a theme, some planted in whitewashed buckets, some pressed and framed. There are dried green hydrangeas, troughs of wheatgrass, fragrant lavender in white and green jugs and huge platters filled with crunchy green apples. The walls are of white painted wood or stone and the styling details are immaculate. There are thoughtful set pieces in every corner made from simple objects associated with water, like mounted fish, vintage swimsuits, lifebuoys and shell-encrusted chests. An amazing stairway leading from the main part of the house to the summer room has a banister rail made of rhododendron twigs (shown on page 55). It was designed and constructed by Buzz Stone of Atlanta, who was also responsible for the fairytale bed in the spare room (see pages 58–59).

Helen has created a look that is achievable, affordable and understated. A lot of her furniture and decorative objects are simple French country, like her zinc-topped dining table and the Pernod water jugs (shown on page 61). She has used collections of shells, stones, insects and old birds' eggs, and is keen on items as disparate as monogrammed linen and beekeeping equipment. Her enthusiasms, and those of her family, have shaped their environment, and that's a real style statement.

left and right AN EXAMPLE OF USING BITS AND PIECES
IN A TOTALLY INSPIRED WAY. HELEN BALLARD WEEKS'S
BATHROOM HAS AN ECLECTIC MIX, FROM COAT RACK
AND PLATE TO HIP FLASK AND GLOVE MANNEQUIN. THE
STRAW BAG AND THE OLD-FASHIONED RED SWIMSUIT
MAKE A WALL DECORATION MORE IN KEEPING WITH THIS
HOUSE THAN ANY WORK OF ART WOULD BE.

top and right IN HELEN BALLARD WEEKS'S LAKESIDE HOME, THE FAMILY ROOM OPENS UP ON ALL SIDES TO THE GARDEN, AND RUSTIC TOUCHES ABOUND. THE MOST STARTLING IS THE RHODODENDRON-TWIG STAIRCASE BANISTER.

above and above right ADDING A TOUCH OF AMERICANA. TWO WAYS TO USE FADED FLAG-INSPIRED FABRICS FROM ANDREW MARTIN OF WALTON STREET: ONE AS A CUSHION AND THE OTHER AS AN UPHOLSTERED SEAT FOR A BATTERED OLD LEATHER CHAIR.

left A STRIKING CEDAR DAISY TABLE
IS THE CENTRE OF ATTENTION IN
THIS RELAXED FAMILY ROOM IN THE
BALLARD WEEKS LAKESIDE HOME.
IT WAS AN INSPIRED ANTIQUES
SHOP FIND AND GOES WELL WITH
THE RATTAN CHAIRS. WHEN IT'S TIME
FOR A NEW LOOK, THE TABLE
STAYS WHERE IT IS WHILE THE SEAT
CUSHIONS GET RECYCLED.
right AN OBJECT LESSON IN STYLING
– A BALANCED ARRANGEMENT OF
SIMPLE THINGS.

overleaf THE SPARE BEDROOM
FEATURES A RHODODENDRON-TWIG
BED. THE ROOM IS FULL
OF PERSONALITY YET IT IS SIMPLE,
RELAXED AND TIMELESS.

above HELEN BALLARD WEEKS GROWS WHEATGRASS
FROM SEED ON SMALL PLASTIC TRAYS AND THEN
PILES IT INTO CONTAINERS. WHEATGRASS IS THE
SIMPLEST AND MOST STYLISH OF HOUSE PLANTS.
right THE DINING ROOM IN THE BALLARD WEEKS HOME.
THE CHAIRS HAVE SLIPCOVERS FOR EVERYDAY USE,
WHILE ON GRANDER OCCASIONS THEY ARE WHIPPED
OFF TO REVEAL ELEGANT WOODEN CHAIRS WITH
UPHOLSTERED SEATS. BETWEEN MEALS THE ZINC-
TOPPED TABLE IS USED TO DISPLAY A COLLECTION OF
FRENCH WATER JUGS FILLED WITH FOLIAGE. THERE IS
TEXTURE EVERYWHERE, BUT THE COLOURS ARE COOL.

TABLES FOR ALL SEASONS

Match the mood of your table to the
mood of the occasion

CREATING A TABLE SETTING is like dressing a set for a one-off performance. It's a temporary, fleeting thing, a chance to bring out favourite pieces that have found their way to the back of the cupboard and to have fun amusing and entertaining your friends. Seasonal fruits and flowers are the natural starting place for dreaming up a scheme, and I like to use them to bring richness to a winter table and to introduce a cool, icy sparkle to my summer tables with the addition of white china and glass. I am always on the lookout for opulent table napkins. My legendary collection includes pleated Fortuny napkins and a set of Indian silk ones that I team up with plain napkins, tying them together and pulling them though a napkin ring. I scour antique shops and flea markets for attractive items of cutlery and it never really bothers me if I can't find a full set, because if you keep looking you can build up a near match, which is often more interesting. I am also lucky in that I have friends who are as acquisitive in this area as I am, and so there's a lot of lending going on which all adds to the fun and to the possibilities.

JESSICA JESSEL'S WINTER TABLE SETTING HAS THE OPULENT
LOOK OF GOLD AND PURPLE. THE ETCHED DECANTER BOTTLES
ARE SIMPLE, EFFECTIVE AND INEXPENSIVE AND LOOK GOOD
WITH EITHER WINE OR WATER.

JESSICA JESSEL HAS THE KNACK OF FINDING INTERESTING
THINGS ON HER TRAVELS OR WHEN BROWSING THROUGH
FLEA MARKETS, PULLING THEM OUT TO USE WITH GREAT
EFFECT FOR HER TABLE SETTINGS. MOST OF THE PIECES
ON THIS TABLE ARE INEXPENSIVE. THE OPULENT-LOOKING
TABLECLOTH, FOR INSTANCE, IS A LENGTH OF
CURTAINING GAUZE FROM THE LONDON DEPARTMENT
STORE PETER JONES.

JESSICA JESSEL HAS AN IMPECCABLE EYE and she always produces the most imaginative table settings. She kindly agreed to devise a summer and winter arrangement for us, in her London apartment, using for both schemes a round table with a velour underskirt in rich tones of grape and juniper. For the winter setting, shown on page 62 and pages 64–65, a glossy gauze cloth was laid over the top. This created an opulent framework for a theme based on glass and burnished gold, inspired perhaps by the gold-rimmed, bronze-coloured plates picked up while on holiday in Provence. The plates were placed on top of gleaming brass chargers which contrast dramatically with the rich purple cloth. The cotton napkins, a lucky find and an exact match, were loosely knotted on the plates. The long-stemmed wine glasses and the decorative decanter bottles shimmer in the light from two ormolu (gilt-bronze) candelabra, as do the glass inner plates with their lovely bobble edges, which would be completely lost if they weren't set off by the gold. Other table details include cut-glass salt cellars and individual glass butter pots. Deliciously and unashamedly theatrical, the effect contrives both to charm and to whet the appetite at first sight.

For the summer table, shown here, a check cloth in a sunny mix of raspberry, carnation pink and white was chosen. This square cloth has been cleverly folded and tied with ribbons at each corner to make it fit snugly and look very stylish and different. In keeping with the berry red theme, the raspberry red plates were placed on damson-coloured underplates. The same elegant, long-stemmed wine glasses and silverware as for the winter setting have been used to add sparkle. The decanter bottles now hold a Provençal rosé, and the crisp linen napkins alternate between strawberry pink and deep plum. In the centre of the table, a single red rose blooms in a beautiful cranberry-coloured bud vase. It is flanked by two burgundy-coloured tole leaves on which perch gold-topped ruby-glass pepper grinders, matching glass salt cellars and feisty scarlet and brass bowls. Like the Provençal plates used on the winter table, the bowls, which serve as butter dishes, were bought on holiday, this time in Cape Town. The table is a glorious profusion of summer-fruit colours, very welcoming and very tasty.

DETAILS OF JESSICA JESSEL'S SUMMER TABLE AND ITS LUSCIOUS BERRY RED COLOUR SCHEME. AGAIN THIS IS A SERENDIPITOUS MIX OF BITS AND PIECES COLLECTED OVER THE YEARS. JESSICA FOUND THE TOLE-LEAF PLATES IN THE OKA MAIL ORDER CATALOGUE, AND THE UNDERPLATES ARE COURTESY OF A HOLIDAY IN MADRID. THE CHECKED TABLECLOTH IS MADE FROM A LENGTH OF JANE CHURCHILL FABRIC AND THE RASPBERRY RED CURVY PLATES ARE FROM THE LONDON DEPARTMENT STORE PETER JONES.

right LOUISE BRADLEY'S TABLE IS CROWDED WITH CANDELABRAS OF THE MOST AMAZING KIND IN WHICH ARMS OF RANDOM HEIGHTS HAVE BEEN FIXED INTO OLD PIECES OF CARVED STONE. AROUND THE BASES OF THE CANDELABRAS SHE HAS MASSED THE LITTLE SQUARE, WHITEWASHED TERRACOTTA POTS KNOWN AS MELON POTS, WHICH WERE USED IN 19TH-CENTURY GREENHOUSES TO GROW EXOTIC FRUITS FROM SEED. left ANOTHER FANTASTIC CANDELABRA FROM LOUISE BRADLEY.

LOUISE BRADLEY HAS CREATED a dramatic setting in the leather-lined apartment shown on pages 48–9. Louise has chosen a simple antique refectory table in a dark wood to echo the dark brown of the leather walls and she has teamed it with high-backed upholstered dining chairs which is a look I predict will soon be seen everywhere. The table is left bare save for a long Irish linen runner down the centre. Antique French candelabras stuck into carved stone bases are tall enough to let diners see through to those sitting opposite and be lit flatteringly from above. The apartment is masculine and this is an appropriately strong, linear table setting. No pretty silver vases filled with roses decorate this table, but white heather planted into old terracotta melon pots. The cutlery is as robust as the rest – serious, chunky and horn-handled. The sparkling glass, the touches of silver and the stylish table china complete this fashionably informal setting.

STUART HANDS IS THE MOST CREATIVE curtain maker I know. He is also the most hospitable of souls, so it seemed an excellent plan to ask him to come up with a selection of creative table settings in his own dining room. Each successive tableau was a marvel of reinvention. The flowers were by Julie Roil of London's Lanesborough Hotel; she worked tirelessly and with enormous imagination. The autumnal red table, shown on pages 70–71, looks as if it has been set up outdoors, thanks to the dappled light that filters down from the tall iron candelabra, through the forest of rosy red eucalyptus leaves. The rustic effect is enhanced by the use of my iron underplates, borrowed for the occasion, and terracotta soup bowls. The delight of this setting is that in spite of the first impression of a forest of trees on the table, the seated diners can see each other perfectly because all of the glorious red foliage creates a bower above their heads.

STUART HANDS'S DRAMATIC AUTUMN TABLE WITH ITS
EMPHASIS ON IRONWORK, LEAF MOTIFS AND STUNNING RED
EUCALYPTUS LEAVES. THE LOVELY NATURAL LINEN
NAPKINS FROM NINA CAMPBELL HAVE BEEN SLIPPED INTO
UNUSUAL IRON NAPKIN RINGS, AND THE CUTLERY IS
UPENDED INTO INDIVIDUAL FLOWERPOTS.

STUART'S SUMMER TABLE IS AS INSPIRING AND DRAMATIC AS IT IS SIMPLE. INDIVIDUAL SUNFLOWER HEADS PROGRESS DOWN THE TABLE, ALTERNATELY PLACED DIRECTLY ON THE SURFACE AND IN GLASSES COVERED IN WIRE. THIS GIVES A STEP UP AND DOWN EFFECT THAT IS MUCH FRIENDLIER THAN A DIVIDING HEDGE, WHICH WOULD BE DEATH TO THE FREE FLOW OF CONVERSATION.

It is hard to believe that Stuart Hands's summer table was laid in the same room as the winter one. The setting has a young, modern look and the chosen menu had an oriental touch, which immediately obviated the need for traditional place settings with knives and forks. There's a lovely ordered, Zen-like look to the table thanks to the line of white napkins marching down the centre and the sharp right-angles of the napkins doubling as place mats. I think the joy of this setting is its simplicity combined with the graphic boldness of the sunflowers.It is such an easy idea to copy, especially as you don't have to restrict the idea to sunflowers. You could use overblown flower heads on their last gasp – there are many flowers that look absolutely wonderful just before they die. The most expensive items on the table are my stylish blue Anthony Stern glasses, loaned for the occasion. It's great when friends can borrow and lend items that you just know will make all the difference.

Delicate and decorative, the white springtime table (see pages 74–75) is covered with a lovely white linen cloth that sweeps the floor. The glassware, not all of it matching, twinkles and invites, but I think the stars of the show are the pansy candles and the glamorous double silk napkins. For the flowers, Julie Roil filled three tall glass vases with giant white delphiniums, and she intertwined Phalaenopsis orchids and agapanthus along the table so it looked like a springtime bower. Delicate glass candlesticks are dotted between the delphiniums, and the effect is artful but simple.

THESE ARE ALL DETAILS FROM STUART HANDS'S LOVELY SPRING TABLE WHICH IS CRISP AND WHITE AND SHIMMERS WITH GLASSWARE. THE SILK NAPKINS ARE, IN FACT, MINE. THE OUTER NAPKINS, WHICH ARE FROM INDIA, ARE EXTREMELY ELEGANT AND MADE OF SILK EMBROIDERED WITH BITS OF GLASS. THEY HAVE TO BE DRY-CLEANED, SO I TWIST EACH ONE TOGETHER WITH A PLAIN SILK NAPKIN IN THE HOPE THAT THE PLAIN NAPKIN IS THE ONE THAT WILL GET USED. THEY ARE TWISTED WITH WHITE BEADS WHICH ARE ACTUALLY A CHEAP CHRISTMAS DECORATION. THE GLASSES ARE LOVELY. THERE ARE THREE DIFFERENT PATTERNS OF ETCHED GLASS ON THIS TABLE – WHICH ALL GOES TO SHOW THAT IT DOESN'T MATTER IF THINGS DON'T MATCH. I THINK THE PANSY CANDLES BORDER ON THE VULGAR, BUT I ABSOLUTELY LOVE THEM IN THIS CONTEXT.

STUNNING AND VERY FESTIVE, STUART'S CHRISTMAS TABLE IS
DESIGNED FOR PEOPLE TO HAVE A GOOD TIME. I THINK IT IS AN
INSPIRED IDEA TO USE CHRISTMAS TREE DECORATIONS ON A
TABLE. THE CUT-OPEN POMEGRANATES ARE ACTUALLY PAPIER-
MÂCHÉ DECORATIONS FROM MEXICO, AND LOOK TEMPTINGLY
LIKE THE REAL THING.

Stuart's Christmas table is a feast for the eye. No tablecloth was used, so the glowing wood provided the perfect background for the collection of red, gold and green ornaments piled generously into the centre. Three different suites of glasses were used, all of them Stuart's own. Two are clear and one was Bristol green, perfect for Christmas, and best used just for water, as green doesn't do justice to the ruby hues of wine. There are live green trees in little tubs, which look very sweet with the delicious baubles piled at their feet like heaps of irresistible gifts. The tartan napkins, a perfect touch, are from Ann Gish of California and the glass plates holding the individual Christmas desserts are my mother's. The spectacular quartet of silver candlesticks gave the table a real wow factor.

THE CENTREPIECE OF MY AUTUMN family wedding breakfast buffet forms part of the transformation scene of my blue and white kitchen described on page 14 and pictured on pages 12–13 and 78–79. Obviously this is not a table set for dining, but it does illustrate how wonderfully fruit and flowers complement the food, glass, china and silverware in a setting, and in fact the extravagant flowers made the food nestled in the undergrowth look that much more inviting.

It would be easy to imagine from looking at these splendid settings for feasts, that a well-decorated table leaves no room for the food. It is a great idea to load the centre of the table with serving dishes so people can help themselves, and this is the ideal thing to do for family meals, but for special occasions the sight of half-empty bowls and platters may not create the right ambience. The French, of course, have a perfect way of coping with the service of food: they produce a *table de service*, a small portable table which appears miraculously laden with each new culinary offering and onto which plates and dishes can be cleared between courses. My version of this is a folding garden table which, covered with an appropriate cloth, gets whisked in and out and nobody really notices its presence.

THIS TRIUMPHANT TABLE SETTING WAS MEANT TO LOOK AS DELICIOUSLY OVER THE TOP AS POSSIBLE. I PULLED OUT EVERYTHING I HAD THAT WOULD GIVE THE TABLE SHEEN AND SPARKLE, FROM THE CLEAR ANTHONY STERN GOBLETS AND CHAMPAGNE BUCKET TO MY MOTHER-OF-PEARL PLATES, THE SILVER SWAN AND THE GORGEOUS OPALINE GLASS FRUIT STANDS. THE MOUTHWATERING COLOUR, OF COURSE, COMES FROM THE AMAZING FRUIT AND FLOWER ARRANGEMENTS BY ROBBIE HONEY.

WINDOWS ON STYLE

Big and bold or neat and discreet, windows are a major focal point

THE CHOICE OF WINDOW TREATMENT IS A BIG DECISION that can make or break a room, because as you enter, your eyes are drawn to the source of light. There are a wealth of choices to be made, from framing that source of light with sumptuous drapes that swagger confidently to the floor, to discreetly veiling it with a tailored blind, and in this chapter we are going to explore some of them. Changing a window treatment is a dramatically quick fix for any room because you can use curtaining to alter the perception of proportion in the same way that a change of clothes can alter the perception of a person. You can make the windows appear taller and thinner or wider and shorter, and you can either draw attention to them or make them blend into the background. Of course, curtains can be an expensive item, and not something you want to change with the seasons, but you can add and subtract in subtle ways that make all the difference, rather like adding a new twist to a favourite old outfit.

above SOMETIMES A WINDOW IS TOO PRETTY TO COVER
UP, IN WHICH CASE ALL IT NEEDS IS AN ORCHID.
right THESE ARE MY AMAZING ORGANZA AND PASHMINA
CURTAINS. SINCE I HAD THE ORGANZA BLIND MADE FOR
ME FROM FABRIC SUBTLY PAINTED WHITE ON WHITE BY
COLLEEN BERY, I TEND TO LEAVE THEM FALLING STRAIGHT.

PELMETS ARE USED ORNAMENTALLY to top a window treatment and practically to hide the curtain track. The pelmet on page 80 is a pelmet like no other. It is in the main bedroom of the London apartment of Zein Al Naqib, an enthusiastic and knowledgeable collector of textiles and costume. The designer Louise Bradley found a craftsman to make this stunning confection after Zein showed her a photograph of a Venetian glass pelmet. It is an inspired touch and goes perfectly with the luxurious quilted Porthault fabric curtains over voile sheers with insets of exquisite lace. The over-long curtains rest heavily on the floor without falling into puddles. It is quite a critical decision getting the over-long look just right, and when it works, as it does here, it adds to the sense of opulence.

MY PASHMINA AND ORGANZA CURTAINS give me nothing but pleasure. You can see them in the context of my bedroom transformation on pages 26–27, but they are so good that they deserved a close-up all to themselves. I did not have to buy dozens of pashmina shawls, as Bernie de Le Cuona helpfully sells pashmina by the yard (metre) in every shade of white and beige, and for a hard-wearing, lightweight, stunning fabric it is hard to find an equal. Stuart Hands made these curtains for me with organza inner curtains and pashmina next to the window. I like the way they hang freely fluttering in the breeze, but when I want to change the look, I pull back the pashmina curtains and loop the organza curtains with a pair of silk and linen tassels by Wendy Cushing. These look just perfect as they are not too silky.

Organza is an ideal material for blinds, too. It's there but not there, obscuring an ugly view or maintaining privacy very subtly. Colleen Bery has used organza blinds in her bathroom, but first took the precaution of painting an all-over pattern directly onto the organza to obscure the view further.

far left WHEN I DO TIE BACK MY BEDROOM CURTAINS, I LOOP UP THE ORGANZA CURTAIN WITH A SIMPLE LINEN TIE-BACK AND TASSEL, LEAVING THE HEAVIER, PASHMINA LAYER HANGING GRACEFULLY TO THE FLOOR.
left COLLEEN BERY'S BATHROOM HAS ONE OF HER OWN HAND-PAINTED ORGANZA BLINDS AT THE WINDOW FOR PRIVACY WITHOUT LOSS OF LIGHT.

far left A PAINTED BLIND AND SWAGS, PAINTED AND MADE BY BERY DESIGNS, DRESS THE SMALL WINDOW IN ZEIN AL NAQIB'S BATHROOM. left UNLINED FORTUNY SILK CURTAINS LET IN A SHIMMER OF LIGHT TO HELEN BALLARD WEEKS'S ATLANTA, GEORGIA, HOME. below far left A HIGH TIE-BACK GIVES THESE DRAWING ROOM CURTAINS A TALL, ARCHITECTURAL ELEGANCE. below left CONVERSELY, A LOW TIE-BACK MAKES THESE BEDROOM CURTAINS LOOK EXPANSIVE AND GENEROUS. right ONE OF MY HALL CURTAINS. THERE'S ANOTHER ONE ON THE OTHER SIDE OF THE CABINET. THEY ARE MADE UP OF THREE LAYERS OF CURTAIN, THE OUTER LAYER OF WHICH HAS CHANGED FROM RED CHENILLE TO A HAND-PAINTED TERRACOTTA CLOTH BY COLLEEN BERY.

TIE-BACKS TRANSFORM a straight set of curtains into dramatic sweeps that can enhance an attractive fabric or texture. Using a high tie-back makes a curtain look architectural and smart, while using a tie-back low down makes the curtain look theatrical and generous. On the subject of theatrical effects, the tied and fringed swag of fabric looped over the curtain rail in Zein Al Naqib's bathroom, pictured on page 86, makes the pretty little window look like a miniature stage set for a grand opera. I love the way Helen Ballard Weeks has simply looped back a length of exquisite, unlined Fortuny fabric from the window of her Atlanta townhouse – it's a fabulously extravagant gesture.

COLLEEN BERY'S DAUGHTER BRYONY wanted to design her own blinds and make a virtue of the dormer window in her bedroom by turning it into a canopy using a clever mechanism that sweeps the blind up over the ceiling of the dormer. She's teamed bold, modern stripes with a white on white formal pattern on the bedspread. It's bright and modern and very arresting.

Colleen's hand-painted curtains frame a window seat in her sitting room (see page 92). They are dress curtains and are not intended to be opened or closed, so they've been tied back high enough to allow unimpeded passage. Falling from a magnificent painted wood pelmet, the fabric has been twisted around brass rosettes so that the lower part of each curtain reveals a rich red lining. It makes a wonderfully inviting alcove and luckily overlooks an enclosed garden, so being unable to close the curtains does not become an issue.

THE TALL, WIDE WINDOWS IN DANIELLE MOUDABBER'S
APARTMENT ARE GIVEN THE MINIMALIST TREATMENT WITH
SIMPLE, ELECTRICALLY OPERATED BLINDS WHICH LEAVE
THE ROOM FREE TO EXPRESS ITSELF.

this page THE DRESS CURTAINS IN COLLEEN
BERY'S SITTING ROOM FRAME A WINDOW
SEAT OVERLOOKING THE GARDEN.
THESE ARE CURTAINS USED PURELY AS
AN ARCHITECTURAL FEATURE, ADDING
IMPORTANCE TO THE OPENING.
right THE BALLARD WEEKS GARDEN ROOM,
WHERE NO CURTAINS ARE REQUIRED.

THE GRAND WINDOWS IN DANIELLE MOUDABBER'S apartment (see pages 30–35) are a reminder that her living room was once a magnificent Victorian ballroom almost 40 feet (12 metres) long, with a ceiling height to match. Consequently, the windows needed dressing down. To do that, Danielle had sleek white roller blinds (shown on pages 90–91) made so the windows fade into the wall and all attention is focused on the wonderful collections of art and furniture that Danielle has put together. Light still shines through when the blinds are down, which is fine for a living room but not so sleep-inducing for a bedroom.

ENCLOSED GARDENS SURROUNDING LIVING AREAS ensure privacy from prying eyes and if you have beautiful windows or glass doors it is a shame to dress them up unnecessarily. Helen Ballard Weeks has taken this line with the sitting room in her Atlanta townhouse. There are so many lovely things to catch the eye that curtains would be a step too far and would get in the way of the magnificent ever-changing views of the garden. This room goes through its seasonal changes in style thanks to Mother Nature.

NEAT BLINDS OFFER A TAILORED SOLUTION to window dressing. They use far less fabric but can deliver as much impact as curtains. Danielle Moudabber has gone for drama in her bedroom with hand-painted purple lightproof blinds and simple royal blue curtains. The floral fabrics of Andrew Martin of Walton Street are as far away from the traditional view of chintz as it is possible to get.

right DANIELLE MOUDABBER'S LIGHTPROOF BEDROOM
BLINDS WERE DESIGNED AND MADE BY SARAH MAYNARD,
WHO NOW DESIGNS CARS.
far right THIS SIMPLE ROLLER BLIND IS CROWDED WITH
TULIPS, WHILE THE COMPLEMENTARY FABRIC ON THE
SLIPCOVER TAKES THE THEME A LITTLE MORE CALMLY. BOTH
FABRICS ARE BY ANDREW MARTIN OF WALTON STREET.

PRETTY AS A PICTURE

Change the look and feel of a room by moving
pictures and paintings, rearranging groups of images
or adding to existing collections

THE IMAGES ON YOUR WALLS should give you constant pleasure day in day out. Choose pictures to please yourself, not just because they are going to appreciate in value or because there's a rumour going round that something is fashionable. A good way to start when hanging pictures is to gather together the images you want in a certain room and then think of the room as a whole rather than each picture in isolation. It's useful to remember that it is the room you are decorating, not the pictures you are displaying, unless of course you happen to run an art gallery! Where to hang them will gradually become clear as you move around the room. Keep in mind the angles your pictures will be seen from, and look out for areas of wall that would benefit from a splash of colour or a strong linear or horizontal arrangement.

A BIT OF WIT ALWAYS GOES DOWN WELL when hanging pictures. Stuart Hands and David Cowdery had a portrait painted of their dog sitting in her favourite chair, and they placed the portrait on the wall directly behind the chair. This produces an amusing double-take as Cornflake spends a lot of her time posing in her chair, hoping to inspire more works of art.

left ON THE NARROW WALLS ON EITHER SIDE OF THE WINDOW IN MY BEDROOM I HAVE ARRANGED COLUMNS OF ORIGINAL COSTUME DESIGNS BY YOLANDA SONNABEND. THEY ARE DESIGNS FOR OPERA AND BALLET COSTUMES FOR PRODUCTIONS AT COVENT GARDEN, LA SCALA AND THE LIKE. THE DESIGNS I PICKED WERE ALL BLUE, AND THEY WERE ALL FOR MALE COSTUMES. THEY FRAME MY WINDOW BEAUTIFULLY. right THIS IS A COLLECTION OF ANGELS, OR PUTTI, ON A NARROW WALL BETWEEN TWO WINDOWS IN MY GALLERY. THE SUBJECT MATTER IS ALL THE SAME, BUT THE FRAMES MAKE A MOSAIC OF DIFFERING SHAPES AND COLOURS. THE PRINTS, ETCHINGS AND DRAWINGS RANGE IN AGE FROM 17TH CENTURY TO 20TH.

COLLECTIONS OF PICTURES of the same subject matter, but of different shapes and sizes and in a variety of frames, can look wonderful if you treat the collection as a whole. At one stage I had a lovely collection of drawings and engravings of angels in my gallery in a medley of decorative gilded frames, which you can see on page 99. I grouped them on a wall between two windows, putting the strongest drawing in the centre, at eye level, and letting the others crowd around in an ordered but not symmetrical way. They filled the wall and, as they were hung on the wall facing the door, made a memorable impact. You can see too how I picked the frames to go with the cream and blue of the hand-embroidered curtains.

As themed collections go, I really like Kate Bannister's approach. Kate is an antiques dealer and you can see some of her collections here. She has made a corner of the dining area of her kitchen into a gallery of pictures of houses in wooden frames, calling the collection 'The Council Estate'. They are absolutely charming and repay close scrutiny. You don't always need a wall to show off images, however. Zein Al Naqib wanted to introduce a bit of classical style into the second bathroom of her London home, and she did this by finding an early Victorian wooden screen and replacing its dark lacquered panels with architectural prints in sepia on a white ground. It looks stunning.

NOT EVERYTHING YOU HANG ON A WALL HAS TO BE A PICTURE. I like to also hang pieces of carved wood that are fragments of wooden overdoors. Dating from around the eighteenth century, overwoors were made to decorate the space above internal doors and below the cornice. I find that a piece of carved wood can really tie together a collection of pictures.

above KATE BANNISTER'S COLLECTION OF PICTURES OF HOUSES. SINGLY THEY
WOULD NOT HAVE MUCH TO SAY BUT GROUPED TOGETHER THEY HAVE IMPACT.
above right ZEIN AL NAQIB'S BATHROOM SCREEN DISPLAYS IMAGES OF THE GRAND
HOUSES AND STONE HALLS OF COLONIAL ARCHITECTURE.
right THIS ARRANGEMENT IS TO BE FOUND IN MY LIBRARY AT HOME. THE IMAGES
ALL RELATE TO THE CENTRAL THEME OF INTERIORS PAST AND PRESENT.

On page 101 you can see another arrangement from the library at my home. I've used a carved garland to hold together some lovely paintings of interiors grouped around a pretty little watercolour, one of the earliest depictions of an elevator, in a beautiful hand-made frame.

I'VE ALWAYS LOVED PLACING PICTURES ON BOOKSHELVES. It invariably looks good to see books and pictures interspersed, but I think the pictures look best randomly propped on small easels or leaning against the books. In fact, an ordered randomness is what I try to achieve for every collection of pictures that I hang. I use mantels and shelves too, making the pictures and objects propped against the wall part of the impact. In my bathroom, shown on pages 102–103, I have a triptych of shapely urns flanked by angels, with a supporting cast of family photos, drawings and silhouettes on a shelf beneath.

HANGING LARGE, INDIVIDUAL PICTURES is not difficult. Impressive paintings, icons, mirrors or montages are designed to be a focal point, drawing the eye as you enter the room. And this is precisely why changing your pictures around is such a good, quick way to change the character of your room.

HANGING COLLECTIONS of prints, pictures or photos, on the other hand, is not so easy. You can align various elements by either the bottoms, the edges or the tops of the frames, or create a balanced arrangement around a central core. The collection of black and white photos and drawings in Danielle Moudabber's apartment shown on page 106 is a case in point. Here the pictures on the left of the group have been hung on a vertical axis, and those on the right on a horizontal, making the space between the images as pleasing to the eye as the pictures themselves.

And speaking of a vertical alignment, just look at the impact of a strip of Andy Warhol 'Marilyn' wallpaper pasted onto Danielle's hall cupboard door, pictured on page 107. With the door open, the images can be glimpsed from the sitting room, and when closed, they give her classically proportioned Victorian hall a real boost.

It takes a real talent to hang rows of virtually identical pictures without them looking boring, and Helen Ballard Weeks has succeeded admirably with her collection of pressed flowers, displayed above a sideboard in her lakeside home. The frames are as simple as the planked walls, and the inspired touch of the visible nails and cords gives the group a dynamic diagonal element, linking the pictures together well.

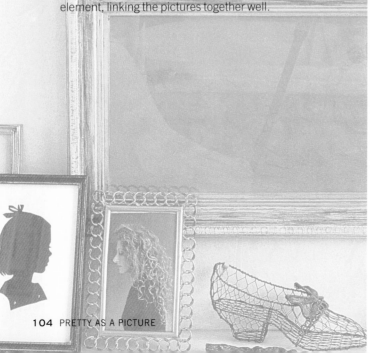

previous pages THE SHELF IN MY BATHROOM SERVES A DUAL PURPOSE: IT HIDES THE PLUMBING AND IS A REPOSITORY FOR A COLLECTION OF SILHOUETTES AND PHOTOGRAPHS THAT RELATE TO THE DRAWINGS ON THE WALL BEHIND. THE ANGELS FLANKING THE URNS ARE 17TH-CENTURY SANGUINE DRAWINGS.

right THIS WALL IN HELEN BALLARD WEEKS'S HOME IS AN ARTFUL ARRANGEMENT OF IMAGES AND OBJECTS SHE HAS GATHERED THAT WORK WELL TOGETHER.

above THE STRIKING COLLECTION OF BLACK AND WHITE FRAMED PHOTOGRAPHS IN DANIELLE MOUDABBER'S HALLWAY. THERE'S NO RIGIDITY ABOUT THIS ARRANGEMENT, AND IT LEAVES PLENTY OF SCOPE FOR ADDITIONS. IN FACT, SHE HASN'T USED PHOTOGRAPHS EXCLUSIVELY: I LOVE THE ACCENT OF THE DRAWING ON THE TOP RIGHT CORNER.
right ANDY WARHOL'S 'MARILYN' DECORATES THE INSIDE OF DANIELLE'S COAT CUPBOARD, EMPHASIZING THE SILVER HIGHLIGHTS ON THE VICTORIAN PANELLING IN HER HALLWAY.

SOME WONDERFUL TOUCHES FROM
THE HOME OF ZEIN AL NAQIB. ON HER
BEDROOM WALL SHE HAS PLACED FOUR
EXQUISITE 18TH-CENTURY MIRROR
FRAMES, BUT LEFT THEM EMPTY. THE
EFFECT IS MARVELLOUSLY ENIGMATIC.
right A PLAYFUL CORNER DOMINATED BY
A PORTRAIT ON A CUSHION. YOU CAN
SEE HERE HOW A TOTALLY ECLECTIC
COLLECTION OF PICTURES CAN WORK
WELL TOGETHER IF THE PICTURES ARE
THOUGHTFULLY BALANCED.

FRAMES MAKE ALL THE DIFFERENCE, giving status to the simplest drawing and affecting the way you look at any picture. I recommend searching flea markets and second-hand stores and keeping a cache of interesting frames to hand just in case you find something to fit. You can often find them in interesting shapes that were presumably made to fit long-forgotten amateur watercolours, family portraits or pictures of ships. Old frames are expensive to restore and paint, but I actually like frames that look a bit battered and distressed. In fact, frames can sometimes be more interesting than the pictures they surround. Some frames are so stunning that they don't need pictures in them at all. Zein Al Naqib has hung four gorgeous empty frames on her bedroom wall and they look like works of art in their own right (see page 108).

Zein has also created a witty arrangement on a dark panelled wall above a little sofa (see page 109), using the jewel-like colours of the cushions to accentuate the colours in the central naive floral painting. She has three portraits in this grouping – the fact that one of them is on a cushion just adds to the whimsy. The collection of crystal intaglio in the delightfully eccentric wooden frame at the eye-catching centre of the arrangement is an example of decorative imagery at its most striking. You can have virtually anything mounted and framed, from baby's first boot to grandfather's collection of beetles. It is fun to create one's own installations of family memorabilia in a shallow frame just by fixing a shallow box with shelves into a frame. Or if you have a pretty collection of any items, be they old buttons or silver lockets, do consider creating a frame and hanging them up for all to admire. I've successfully framed all kinds of pretty things, from red wax seals to Indian playing cards.

THERE'S A MODERN TAKE ON COLLECTIONS of personal memorabilia on the wall of Rita Konig's kitchen, shown opposite. Rita, an interior designer, has only one camera, a black and white Polaroid. The stunning wall, which started with just one or two pictures, is, of course, endlessly fascinating to Rita's friends and family, because they all feature in it. But thanks to the arrangement, and the content, unframed monochrome snaps of the same size, it has developed into a strong decorative feature.

THE POLAROID COLLECTION IN THE DESIGNER RITA KONIG'S KITCHEN. A JOYFUL IDEA THAT STARTED SMALL, IT HAS NOW CREPT INTO THE OPEN SHELVING. SOMEHOW IT MAKES THE BOWLS, THE GLASSES AND THE CLASSY ESPRESSO MACHINE LOOK LIKE OBJETS D'ART.

6

FIREPLACES

Playing with the perspectives and moods
of a room's focal point

TO MAKE A FUNDAMENTAL CHANGE to the feel of a living room you need do no more than take a long, hard look at the fireplace. Nowhere else in this book do I advocate calling in the builders and all the disruption that comes with them, but this is the one exception I would make, because a new fireplace can make a monumental difference to a room. I know, because I've done it, and while it does entail a certain amount of mess and disruption, for such a major change it is relatively inexpensive and the transformation takes only a day or two.

Many fireplaces in period houses are too small and too upright. They may have gone well with the small, upright furniture of the day, but they do nothing for the lower, more expansive lines of modern furniture. Of course, there's a lot you can do with accessories, mirrors, pictures and wall colour to improve proportions, and we will be covering these cosmetic changes in this chapter. But if the cosmetics don't work for you, then I have no hesitation in advocating surgery.

THE FIREPLACE AND SURROUNDING PLASTERWORK IN
DANIELLE MOUDABBER'S CUTTING-EDGE APARTMENT WAS A
STYLISTIC ODDITY AMONG THE ART DECO, THE MODERN
FURNITURE AND THE WONDERFULLY STRONG PAINTINGS.
TO PULL THEM TOGETHER, DANIELLE ASKED JANE POPE, WHO
SPECIALIZES IN SILVER LEAF, TO TURN THE FIREPLACE
INTO A WORK OF ART IN ITS OWN RIGHT.

AN UGLY FIREPLACE WITH A DOMINATING OVERMANTEL was part of the Victorian ballroom Danielle Moudabber bought to convert into a home. You can see her wonderful apartment on the right. Her bold decision was not to take the fireplace out but to transform it with silver leaf. Now a stunning, elaborate statement, it holds its own in a room otherwise filled with Art Deco and ethnic works of art. The silver leaf works well with the white walls, as it's not in the least heavy, and the sparkle blends in to the eclectic environment rather than shouting for attention.

Danielle has kept the mantel casual and clear of clutter, preferring a pair of decorative flower-patterned jars, a small mask on a perspex (Plexiglas) base and one tall, shapely vase. The mantel is not a shrine to a fixed set of objects, but a place to display current favourites and even reading matter. This is a fireplace that definitely needs a mirror over it, both to mark it as an architectural feature running the full height of the room and to reflect light from the magnificent full-height windows.

THE FIREPLACE IN THE UPSTAIRS LIVING ROOM OF MY GALLERY in London's Walton Street is shown in various guises on pages 116–119. Walton Street is a terrace of four-storey eighteenth-century houses, which are not at all grand but are well-proportioned and very charming. As I sell decorative pictures, I like to display them in a domestic setting rather than an art gallery environment. I have therefore retained the drawing room feel of the premises, lining the walls with a neutral hessian-weave wallpaper that complements all pictures, whether fresh and bright or dark and glowing.

The obvious way to dress a fireplace is with a traditional portrait or mirror. This invites either a safe, classic form of decoration or something completely louche. The traditional portrait I chose (see page 118) is by the Belgian artist Thierry Poncelet. Thierry buys good, period ancestral paintings and then changes the human head into a dog's head of your choice – the idea is to represent the aristocratic ancestor of your dog rather than your dog itself. The anthropomorphic dogs usually end up looking uncannily like a member of the family. I didn't hang the picture in the conventional way, but just propped it up on the uncluttered mantel, which adds to the unexpected response you get from this painting.

Moving on from the traditional, albeit with a twist, I created a completely different effect with a collection of four paintings of sexy fat ladies painted by the talented artist Lorioz, a petite French woman who always paints ladies larger than life.

THE STARBURST MIRRORS THAT NOW BRIGHTEN UP THE
FIREPLACE WALL OF MY GALLERY IN LONDON'S WALTON
STREET. THIS KIND OF HORIZONTAL ARRANGEMENT
MAKES A FIREPLACE WALL LOOK WIDER.

above THIERRY PONCELET'S 'ARISTOCHIEN' PORTRAIT OF AN
AIREDALE TERRIER IN A FAUX TORTOISESHELL FRAME. THE ORIGINAL
PAINTING WAS PROBABLY LATE 17TH CENTURY OR EARLY 18TH.
right A COLLECTION OF ORIGINAL ACRYLIC PAINTINGS BY LORIOZ.
THE CRYSTAL GLOBE IS, IN FACT, A BANISTER KNOB AND THE LITTLE
EASEL-SHAPED MIRROR IS A CHARMING PIECE FROM THE 1930S.

This collection of embonpoint in the lovely hand-painted frames gave the room a younger, funkier feel, and I cluttered up the mantel with an artfully arranged collection of tortoiseshell and crystal to link the colours of the marble fire surround with the skin tones of the delightfully rotund figures. I hung them so that they would, literally, give the fireplace extra girth.

THE MOST DRAMATIC TRANSFORMATION, seen on pages 116–117, was the next one. I took down the fat ladies and installed a collection of gilded starburst mirrors, some with flat glass and some with convex. They made the room seem wider, and by reflecting light in all sorts of unexpected ways, added a feeling of space. This time I dressed the mantel with upright, right-angled shapes: gilded frames that sparkled and caught the light and leather-bound books to add warmth and gravitas.

You can see from these transformations that a fireplace can become a bold vertical statement, with a large mirror or picture that echoes the dimensions and hues of the mantel carrying the eye up to the ceiling and giving an instant sense of drama. On the other hand, a horizontal grouping of small, related pictures will keep attention focused on the wall as a whole. Most mantelpieces are a magnet for favourite pictures and objects, invitations, postcards and other bits and pieces that can soon add up to clutter. My policy is to find somewhere else for the clutter and either dress my mantelpiece carefully and deliberately, or clear away the lot and enjoy the negative space.

THE TRANSFORMATION UNDERGONE BY THE FIREPLACE IN MY DRAWING ROOM. IT WENT FROM UPTIGHT EDWARDIAN (THIS PAGE) TO GENEROUS PILLARED STONE (RIGHT) IN A COUPLE OF DAYS. A TRICK I LEARNED FROM THE DESIGNER NINA CAMPBELL IS TO TUCK TWO TINY CHAIRS ON EITHER SIDE, AS PEOPLE ARE ALWAYS DRAWN TO SIT NEAR A FIRE.

THE DRAWING ROOM IN MY CHELSEA APARTMENT had an uptight carved wood Edwardian mantel and a dark cast-iron hole of a fireplace that I never liked (see page 120). Whatever I did to the walls and however pretty the objects on the mantel, the proportions of the fireplace and the style did nothing to enhance the room. So I decided to change it. It did not take very long, and it was not particularly messy or expensive, and it is a makeover I am entirely happy with. I chose an early nineteenth-century stone mantel from London's Chiswick Fireplaces and had the opening in the wall enlarged to fit it. The new opening was lined with rough bricks and cement, so I got some talented trompe l'oeil paint specialists to transform it into convincing slabs of York stone, and it looks absolutely lovely. My new fireplace, pictured on page 121, has completely transformed the look of the room. It is lower, paler and wider, and makes the room look substantially bigger.

To complete the transformation, I moved the lovely sixteenth-century portrait in its gilded frame, which gave a bit of a lift to the Edwardian mantel, and installed a sixteenth-century Venetian canvas panel that had previously hung on the other side of the room above a settee. The academic biblical subject matter of soaring pillars was perfect above my pillared mantelpiece. With its honey-coloured hues and curvaceous shape (the original painting was made as an inset to an elaborate wall decoration in a palazzo or a church), it suited the new fireplace wall perfectly. I felt the mantel needed dressing like a nineteenth-century library, so I used a collection of little leather-bound books and short iron candlesticks.

FIREPLACES IN BEDROOMS are rarely used for their original purpose and most people box them in and forget about them. But there are occasions, particularly in period rooms with generous proportions, when it is a good idea to let them be. In the photograph on the right, you can see how the fireplace has been blended into the white walls and makes a splendid plinth for a magnificent overmantel mirror. The fireplace opening itself can be adorned in summer with flowers and in winter with appropriate seasonal foliage or a crackling fire, giving the room an alcove for all seasons. Very quick chic.

A BEDROOM FIREPLACE PROVIDES A FOCAL POINT OTHER THAN THE BED, WHICH GIVES YOU TWO GREAT OPPORTUNITIES FOR INSTANT FIXES: DRESS THE BED DIFFERENTLY AND/OR CHANGE THE WAY YOU ADORN THE MANTEL OR THE FIREPLACE.

THE LOGS, THE FIRE IRONS AND THE LITTLE STOOL
ALL SAY RUSTIC. IF YOU ADDED BOOKS AND A FEW
COSY CHAIRS YOU'D HAVE A LIBRARY.

MORE BALLARD WEEKS FIREPLACE GENIUS. ON THE LEFT IS A MOOSE'S HEAD
DATING FROM THE 1900S. ABOVE LEFT, WE HAVE A COW SKULL THAT LOOKS VERY
COUNTRY. FOR THE TOWNHOUSE (ABOVE), HELEN DECIDED AGAINST ANIMAL
TROPHIES AND USED A CLOCK FACE FOUND IN A FLEA MARKET.

COUNTRY HOUSE fireplaces were meant to be massive structures, dominating a room with their promises of warmth and succour. In times gone by, the lord of the manor would have had his family crest carved ostentatiously into the overmantel so that no visitor could be in doubt of their host's importance and generosity. Luckily, times have changed. The fireplace shown on pages 124–125 is almost the size of a small room but it has a lovely, unpretentious, rustic feel to it that is enhanced by the flanking log shelves. The massive fireplace on pages 128–129, on the other hand, has modern urban chic written all over it, from the stylish lamps to the choice of art.

COUNTRY COTTAGE fireplaces convey their rustic charm on a smaller scale. In the lakeside home of Helen Ballard Weeks, the stone-built chimney in the dining area would be a stunning focal point even if left bare of decoration. The addition of a magnificent moose head is a traditional touch that reminds us this is a house deep in the heart of hunting country.

The fireplace in the family room of Helen's Atlanta townhouse (shown above right) is simplicity itself. The paint and plaster have been hacked away from the brickwork; a plain, solid wooden shelf serves as a mantel and the antique clock face and whitewashed buckets of ferns are robust and simple. I like the way the pretty little antique chair has been upholstered in a fresh check. Just looking at this arrangement of wall, fireplace, mantelshelf and upholstered chair, you can almost ring the changes in your mind's eye. By altering all, or even just one, of the elements, you alter the entire character of the room.

THE ORIGINAL FIREPLACE IN THIS PERIOD HOME WAS
TAKEN OUT AND REPLACED WITH SOMETHING MUCH
LOWER, CLEANER AND MORE MODERN, WHICH PERFECTLY
SUITS THE LOW-SLUNG LINES OF THE MODERN
FURNITURE AND THE STUNNING ARTWORKS.

COLLECTIONS

It's not what your collection consists of that counts;
it's how, and where, you display it

MOST PEOPLE ARE COLLECTORS. Even the purest minimalist among us would concede that if there is beauty in one white pebble, several white pebbles would be all the more striking. You may have some beautiful things hidden away that you would like to display and enjoy, but you are fearful of cluttering the place up. This is where the art of display comes in: it is a question of editing the collectibles, creating witty juxtapositions and showcasing them in a way that ensures the whole is greater than the sum of its parts.

Collections are easy to change and swap around, making them ideal candidates for the quick fix. You can move components within the collection, add or subtract to it – or consign the whole artful arrangement to the back of a cupboard and introduce something completely new. Whichever you do, you will be amazed at the difference it makes to your perception of a space. The eye that is used to alighting on a massive bowl of colourful wooden fruit will be delightfully surprised and refreshed to find in its place a sparkling forest of glass candlesticks. And vice versa.

PAPIER-MÂCHÉ SHOES BY MARIAPIA AND MARINELLA
ANGELINI, A PAIR OF CREATIVE SISTERS WITH AN EXPERTISE
IN FASHION AND ALL THINGS THEATRICAL. DISPLAYED
TOGETHER IN A BATTERED FRAME, THE FANTASY SHOES
HINT AT MUCH MORE THAN THEY WOULD APART.

above left EVEN THE WORKING PARTS OF HELEN BALLARD
WEEKS'S KITCHEN LOOK STUNNING. THIS CUPBOARD
STORES THE CHINA THAT IS USED EVERY DAY.
above and right IN WILLIAM YEOWARD'S WONDERFUL LONDON
SHOP, YEOWARD SOUTH, I FOUND THIS GORGEOUS CABINET
DISPLAYING PORCELAIN BY STEPHANIE HERRING.

CABINETS ARE THE MOST TRADITIONAL WAY to display beautiful bits and pieces. However, when it came to showcasing a collection of exquisite papier-mâché shoes made by the talented Italian sisters Mariapia and Marinella Angelini, I thought some special attention was required. I had an early nineteenth-century Italian frame that had seen better days, and in fact had lost a chunk of carving somewhere along the line, but its elegant, distressed look appealed to me. I asked the gilder Antonio Scialo to turn it into a three-dimensional frame, which he did by adding a back, sides and shelves. I think it works wonderfully well, conjuring up images of masked Venetian ladies tripping off in unsuitable shoes to decadent parties.

While we were photographing Helen Ballard Weeks's home in Atlanta, I couldn't help but admire the lovely French armoire in her breakfast room. The white plates and dishes – a mixture of old plates bought in France and new ones from Smith & Hawkins – are interspersed with stone cabbages, oyster platters and a creamware jug full of horn-handled knives. The result is that a collection of crockery, used on a daily basis by the family, has been transformed into a decorative feature.

William Yeoward is a designer and retailer famous for his amazing collections of crystal, chic fabric and furniture, which he uses to create eye-catching vignettes in the homes of his clients. The fabulous cabinet on the right is designed by William Yeoward. The white finish contrasted with the lime green interior is extremely smart and it does justice to the strong shapes of the beautiful porcelain within.

I HAVE COLLECTED THE HAND-BLOWN glassware of Anthony Stern for years, ever since I saw his work exhibited. It was love at first sight for me and I am still using to this day the very first piece of exquisitely designed glass that I ever purchased from him. I have his drinking glasses in cranberry pink, in Bristol blue, in clear and also in amber, and they are a total pleasure to drink from. I have his candlesticks in every shape and size and much more besides.

The cranberry goblets were far too gorgeous to put away in a cupboard, so I displayed the collection on my hall table for a while (see page 8). That was until Anthony's wonderful stripy glass bottles caught my eye (see page 135). I've grouped them in the centre of the table where they are surrounded by richly coloured walls and the sparkle of mirrors and mirror-framed pictures. I used his wonderful giant-sized goblet as the basis for a table setting which you can see in all its glory on pages 12–13 and 78–79, but you can see the goblet in detail in the photograph on page 134. I took care when dressing the table to play up the gilded ball in the base of the goblet and its wonderful Baroque shape, treating the goblet, the items on the table and the flowers as a temporary collection of related objects and colours for the delight of my guests.

DECORATIVE PLATES DESERVE to be admired but, personally, I'd rather see them on shelves than hung directly on a wall. Helen Ballard Weeks collects brown and white transferware, which she has cleverly displayed on informal white shelving, playing up the brown by interspersing the plates with a beetle collection that came into being as a result of her young son's passion for insects. The brown jug holds a fistful of lovely old horn-handled knives, picked up over the years – few of them match, but in this dining room context, they are more appropriate and attractive than a bunch of flowers.

DISPLAYING GLASS is a wonderful challenge because of the potential to use the play of light to add a touch of drama. Windowsills, or tables in front of windows, are always a good place to start. What you don't want is a row of identical pieces – groups work better, preferably made up of pieces of differing heights. Beware of grouping all the tall elements together or making the group look in any way symmetrical – I think glassware collections should look organic and random.

On pages 138–139 you can see my collection of glass candlesticks on a lovely wooden table in front of my drawing room window. I have a lot of candlesticks, and I love to see them all massed together with narrow glass vases. I can change the look of this collection and the feel of the room just by changing the colours of the flowers – imagine how festive they would look with red roses. The twisted white candles are a big favourite: they look so elegant unlit and they burn down in a graceful, organic kind of way. This collection has been built up over the years and many of them have lost their partners. They look much better together than dotted around the place individually, and that, I think, is the benchmark of a collection that works.

previous pages PART OF MY COLLECTION OF
ANTHONY STERN'S AMAZING GLASS. SOME OF THOSE
TALL LATTICINIO VASES HAVE MIRRORED STRIPES.

opposite HELEN BALLARD WEEKS'S COLLECTION OF 19TH-
CENTURY TRANSFERWARE IS MIXED IN WITH MODERN PIECES.

HERE IS MY OPEN-ENDED COLLECTION OF GLASS CANDLESTICKS AND BUD
VASES. I ALWAYS USE WHITE CANDLES – THESE TWISTED ONES FROM
CALIFORNIA ARE MY FAVOURITES – AND THE BUD VASES HOLD ONLY WHITE
ROSES. THE GLASS DISH IS FILLED WITH SLIVERS OF MOTHER-OF-PEARL.

ON SOME OCCASIONS, LESS CAN BE MORE, in particular when the objects you are displaying are as gorgeous as these elegant pleated vases inspired by the designs of the masters of couture pleating, Fortuny and Issey Miyake. The shapes grouped together in the right-hand photograph are carved from wood by Malcolm Martin and they make a stunning trio. Set against a collage of feathers on hand-made paper, they are very now, very today. The restrained curvaceous forms and the absence of colour give the group a tranquil look, and the emphasis on texture adds a frisson of excitement.

These pieces are sculptures in their own right, and so stunning that they would work as one-off decorative pieces, given some good top lighting to emphasize the texture and a contrasting wall colour to do justice to the shapes. And while the purist may baulk at using them as vases, the pleated calico vase, above right, crafted by Laura Callinan, looks wonderful with a bouquet of dried hydrangeas.

COLLECTIONS ON SHELVES give a wall a three-dimensional element. On these pages you can see shelves treated as showcases, crowded with objects that require your minute attention. Kate Bannister's simple wall-hung shelf unit holds part of her collection of things that are not as they seem. There is a biscuit box that looks like a theatre, mushrooms and cherry tarts made of china, a bunch of carrots that is, in fact, a jug and coloured glass chickens on their nests. It's a fascinating, slightly mad collection of oddities that proves collections don't have to be serious. This collection is next to her dining table so the bits and pieces get used all the time and put back in different places. It's a collection that is open-ended and never static.

How about having your shelf made for you, collection and all? The talented Angelini sisters have created charming trompe l'oeil paintings of shelves that look wonderful in kitchens, bathrooms and hallways, adding a positive touch of wit, imagination and deliciously observed retro kitsch. Their eye for detail betrays their origins as set and costume designers in the film industry. Open shelves always give a room depth, and these charming paintings have the same effect. I have even seen one hung on a cupboard door, hinting tantalizingly at what might lie within.

ORDINARY, EVERYDAY THINGS can make great collections too – again, success lies in the display. On pages 144–145, you can see the effect of a mass of cheap and cheerful red lacquered basketware piled on a bamboo tray. It's simple, stunning and expendable when a new look is called for.

above far left A STRAW HEART FILLED
WITH FRESH FLOWERS, A LOVELY TOUCH
FROM KATE BANNISTER.
above left KATE'S COLLECTION OF THINGS
THAT LOOK LIKE SOMETHING ELSE. SHE USES
THESE PLATES AND BOWLS CONSTANTLY,
SO THE SHELFSCAPE IS ALWAYS CHANGING.
Above and left TROMPE L'OEIL SHELVES FROM
THE ANGELINI SISTERS.

overleaf A COLLECTION OF RED LACQUERED
WICKER MAKES A STRONG STATEMENT.
THE BUNCH OF DRIED SEED PODS PROVES
THAT DRIED FLOWERS DON'T ALWAYS HAVE
TO BE PLACED IN VASES.

left ASHANTE WEIGHING SPOONS TURNED INTO A THREE-DIMENSIONAL PICTURE GIVE A SMALL WALL HIGH IMPACT.

above and right LUGGAGE, SUN HATS AND WALKING STICKS – YOU'VE GOT TO KEEP THEM SOMEWHERE, SO WHY NOT ARRANGE THEM IN A PLEASING WAY AND ENJOY THEM?

Helen Ballard Weeks has placed a collection of walking sticks and straw hats by the front door so they can be used as well as admired, and Zein Al Naqib has decorated her guest room with a touch of whimsy – hats and leather suitcases redolent of a journey on the Orient Express. I had a small collection of gold weighing spoons from West Africa that I couldn't think what do do with until Chris Egerton designed this frame for me, and now my market bargain looks rich and rare.

COLLECTIONS WORK IF THEY HAVE A THEME and the theme on pages 148–153 is animal-related. I think the antlers shown in Rita Konig's bathroom (page 148) and Helen Ballard Weeks's sitting room (page 149) excite me the most. The Ballard Weeks collection of old birds' eggs and turtle shells (pages 150–151) fits in perfectly with the brown and cream theme of their house, and the sailfish that soars above their sideboard (page 153) is a reminder of their waterside location.

The popularity of Thierry Poncelet's 'aristochien' portraits prompted me to display a painting by him among a crowd of china dogs (page 152). I think they look both superb and amusing. But one of my very favourite collections is something very simple and elegant: wonderful friends from Zimbabwe gave me twelve ostrich eggs, and all I did was pile them into a wooden bowl (page 152). They give me pleasure every time I look at them.

EVERYONE IS SCOURING THEIR ATTICS FOR OLD ANTLERS THESE
DAYS. THERE'S EVEN A PIERRE FREY FABRIC DECORATED WITH THEM.
HERE WE HAVE TWO LOOKS FOR ANTLERS. ONE SET IN THE DESIGNER
RITA KONIG'S BATHROOM (ABOVE) LOOKS ZANY AND MODERN, WHILE
A WHOLE COLLECTION ON A WOOD PLANK WALL ADDS A TOUCH OF
THE SCOTTISH BARONIAL TO THE BALLARD WEEKS HOME (RIGHT).

TWO TURTLE SHELLS RESCUED FROM A FLEA MARKET STALL FIT IN PERFECTLY WITH THE BROWN AND CREAM SCHEME. IN THE BALLARD WEEKS HOME THE COLLECTIO OF BIRDS' EGGS BELONGED TO HELEN'S GRANDFATHER. IT IS BEAUTIFULLY JUMBLED AND ACCESSIBLE.

above THE SPANIEL IN FULL RIDING HABIT IS BY
THIERRY PONCELET, AND THE CERAMIC DOGS BY
BRENDAN HESMONDHALGH.
right MY COLLECTION OF OSTRICH EGGS IS DISPLAYED
IN A HUGE SALAD BOWL, NEARLY A YARD (METRE)
ACROSS, THAT IS MADE FROM ONE PIECE OF WOOD.
opposite A SAILFISH CAUGHT BY HELEN BALLARD
WEEKS'S GRANDFATHER FLIES ABOVE A SIDEBOARD
CASUALLY DECORATED WITH AN OLD FISHING BASKET.

GET THE LOOK

VENETIAN MIRRORS

UK

Louise Bradley
15 Walton Street
London SW3 2HX
Tel: (01144) 020 7589 1442
Fax: (01144) 020 7589 2009
Email:
enquiries@louisebradley.
demon.co.uk
(see page 158)

Fenwick of Bond Street
63 New Bond Street
London W1S 1RJ
Tel: (01144) 020 7629 9161

Guinevere Antiques Ltd
578 King's Road
London SW6 2DY
Tel: (01144) 020 7736 2917

India Jane
140 Sloane Street
London SW1X 9AY
Tel: (01144) 020 7730 1070

US

Laura Ashley Home
Tel: (001) 888 457 2838
www.lauraashley.com

DECORATIVE CERAMICS

US

James Graham & Sons
1014 Madison Avenue

New York NY10021
Tel: (001) 212 535 5767
Fax: (001) 212 794 2454
Email: info@james
grahamandsons.com

Lin–Weinberg Gallery
84 Wooster Street
New York NY10013
Tel: (001) 212 219 3022
Email: info@linweinberg.com

William Lipton Ltd
27 East 61st Street
New York NY10021
Tel: (001) 212 751 8131

Minnesota Fats
160 West 26th Street
New York NY10001
Tel: (001) 212 366 6981
www.mnfats.com

Moss
146 Green Street
New York NY10012
Tel: (001) 212 226 2190

TABLEWARE

UK

Bombay Duck
231 The Vale
London W3 7QS
Tel: (01144) 020 8749 8001
Fax: (01144) 020 8749 9000
Email:
info@bombayduck.co.uk
www.bombayduck.co.uk

Designers Guild
267–271 King's Road
London SW3 5EN
Tel: (01144) 020 7243 7300
Fax: (01144) 020 7243 7710
www.designersguild.com

The Dining Room Shop
62–64 White Hart Lane
London SW13 0PZ
Tel: (01144) 020 8878 1020
Fax: (01144) 020 8876 2367
www.thediningroomshop.
co.uk

Divertimenti
139–141 Fulham Road
London SW3 6SD
Tel: (01144) 020 7581 8065
Fax: (01144) 020 7823 9429
Mail order: (01144) 020 8246
4300
www.divertimenti.co.uk

Nicole Farhi
17 Clifford Street
London W1X 1RG
Tel: (01144) 020 7494 9051
Fax: (01144) 020 7494 9052

Graham & Greene
7 Elgin Crescent
Notting Hill
London W11 2JA
Tel: (01144) 020 7727 4594
Fax: (01144) 020 7229 9717

Jerry's Home Store
163–167 Fulham Road
London SW3 6SN
Tel: (01144) 020 7581 0909
Fax: (01144) 020 7584 3749

Names in bold indicate people whose work is shown in this book.   International dialling codes are shown in brackets.

Peter Jones
Sloane Square
London SW1W 8EL
Tel: (01144) 020 7730 3434

OKA
Tel: (01144) 0870 160 6002
www.okadirect.com

Renwick & Clarke
190 Ebury Street
London SW1W 8UP
Tel: (01144) 020 7730 8913
Fax: (01144) 020 7730 4508

Selfridges
400 Oxford Street
London W1A 1AB
Tel: (01144) 020 7629 1234
Fax: (01144) 020 7495 8321
www.selfridges.co.uk

Villeroy & Boch Factory Shop
267 Merton Road
London SW18 5JS
Tel: 020 8875 6006

US

Marc Blackwell
225 5th Avenue
Room 1123
New York NY10010
Tel: (001) 212 696 2827
Fax: (001) 212 696 2104
Email: mblackwell@aol.com
www.marcblackwell.com

Crate and Barrel
Tel: (001) 800 996 9960
www.crateandbarrel.com
(plates, glassware and
serving pieces)

MoMA Design Store SoHo
81 Spring Street
New York NY10012
Tel: (001) 800 793 3167

Once Upon a Table
105 Main Street
Chester
New Jersey
NJ07930–2531
Tel: (001) 908 879 2903

Pottery Barn
Tel: (001) 888 779 5176
www.potterybarn.com
(a US-wide source of all kinds
of things to pep up your
dining table)

Martha Sturdy (Retail)
Tel: (001) 604 737 0037
Email:
info@marthasturdy.com
www.marthasturdy.com

GLASS

UK

The Room
158 Walton Street
London SW3 2JL
Tel: (01144) 020 7225 3225

Anthony Stern
Unit 205–206
Avro House
7 Havelock Terrace
London SW8 4AS
Tel: (01144) 020 7622 9463
(available in US at Barneys
New York, www.barneys.com)

William Yeoward
336 King's Road
London SW3 5UR
Tel: (01144) 020 7351 5454
Fax: (01144) 020 7351 9469
www.williamyeowardcrystal.
com
(available in US at Bergdorf
Goodman, 754 5th Avenue,
New York NY10019-2581
Tel: (001) 800 558 1855)

US

Ralph Lauren
Tel: (001) 800 578 7656
(hurricane lamps)

Source Perrier
Tel: (001) 888 543 2804
(hurricane lamps)

LIGHTING

UK

Mark Brazier-Jones
Hyde Hall Barn
Buntingford
SG9 0RU
Tel: (01144) 01763 273599
Fax: (01144) 01763 273410
Email: studio@
brazier-jones.com
www.brazier-jones.co.uk

Charles Edwards
582 King's Road
London SW6 2DY
Tel: (01144) 020 7736 8490
Fax: (01144) 020 7371 5436
www.charlesedwards.com

Anna French
343 King's Road
London
SW3 5ES
Tel: (01144) 020 7351 1126
Fax: (01144) 020 7351 0421

IKEA
2 Drury Way
London NW10 0TH
Tel: (01144) 020 8451 2767
Fax: (01144) 020 8451 2793

London Lighting Co
135 Fulham Road
London
SW3 2RT
Tel: (01144) 020 7589 3612
Fax: (01144) 020 7581 9652

Mr Light
279 King's Road
London SW3 5EW
Tel: (01144) 020 7352 8398
Fax: (01144) 020 7351 3484

Tindle
162–168 Wandsworth
Bridge Road
London SW6 2UQ
Tel: (01144) 020 7384 1485
Fax: (01144) 020 7736 5630

Vaughan
156–160 Wandsworth
Bridge Road
London SW6 2UH
Tel: (01144) 020 7731 3133
Fax: (01144) 020 7736 4350

US

Isamu Noguchi Garden
Museum
3237 Vernon Boulevard
Long Island City
New York NY11106
Tel: (001) 718 204 7088

FABRICS

UK

Bery Designs
157 St John's Hill
London SW11 1TQ
Tel: (01144) 020 7924 2197
www.decorex.com/
berydesigns.html
(hand-painted curtains
and carpets)

Celia Birtwell
71 Westbourne Park Road
London W2 5QH
Tel: (01144) 020 7221 0877
Fax: (01144) 020 7229 7673

Maryse Boxer at Joseph
26 Sloane Street
London SW1 7LQ
Tel/Fax: (01144) 020 7245
9493
(distributes Carolyn
Quartermaine's hand-painted
silks with calligraphy)

Nina Campbell Ltd
9 Walton Street
London
SW3 2JD
Tel: (01144) 020 7225 1011
Fax: (01144) 020 7823 8353

Chelsea Textiles
7 Walton Street
London SW3 2JD
Tel: (01144) 020 7584 0111
Fax: (01144) 020 7584 7170

Bernie de Le Cuona
9–10 Osborne Mews
Windsor
Berkshire
SL4 3DE
Tel: (01144) 01753 830301
Fax: (01144) 01753 620455
(silk, linen and wool mixes in
every colour imaginable)

Pierre Frey
251–253 Fulham Road
London SW3 6HY
Tel: (01144) 020 7376 5599
Fax: (01144) 020 7352 3024

Liberty
214–220 Regent Street
London W1R 6AH
Tel: (01144) 020 7734 1234
Fax: (01144) 020 7573 9876
www.liberty-of-london.com

Andrew Martin of Walton Street
200 Walton Street
London SW3 2JL
Tel: (01144) 020 7225 5100
Fax: (01144) 020 7589 4957
Email: showroom@andrew-
martin.co.uk
(Americana fabrics)

Christopher Norman Inc.
Unit 2–10 Chelsea Harbour
London
SW10 0XE
Tel: (01144) 020 7351 5164

US

Linensnthings
Tel: (001) 800 568 8765
www.linensnthings.com
(readymade slipcovers)

Darva Murray
116 Lafayette Drive #15
Atlanta, GA 30309
Tel: (001) 678 361 3731
(Provençal quilts)

Sethi & Sethi
990 Avenue of the Americas
Suite 15
New York NY10018
Tel: (001) 212 967 1248
sethisethi@aol.com
(bedlinen, table napkins,
beaded and jewelled fabrics)

**BEDLINEN,
BEDCOVERS, FAKE
FUR SPREADS**

UK

Argos
Tel: (01144) 0870 600 2020

Debenhams
Tel: (01144) 020 7408 4444

Freemans catalogue
Tel: 0800 900200
(Betty Jackson collection)

Heirlooms
Arun Business Park
Bognor Regis
West Sussex
PO22 9SX
Tel: (01144) 01243 820252
Fax: (01144) 01243 821174

Names in bold indicate people whose work is shown in this book.   International dialling codes are shown in brackets.

John Lewis
Oxford Street
London W1A 1EX
Tel: (01144) 020 7629 7711
www.johnlewis.co.uk
(Kelly Hoppen bedlinen)

**The Monogrammed
Linen Shop**
168 Walton Street
London SW3 2JL
Tel: (01144) 020 7589 4033
Fax: (01144) 020 7823 7745
www.monogrammedlinen
shop.co.uk

Tobias and the Angel
68 White Hart Lane
London SW13 0PZ
Tel/Fax: 020 (01144) 8878
8902

Wallace Sacks
Impex House
8 Scrubs Lane
London
NW10 6RB
Tel: (01144) 020 8960 6988

The White Company
298–300 Munster Road
London SW6 6BH
Tel: (01144) 020 7385 7988
Fax: (01144) 020 7385 2685

US

Bed, Bath and Beyond
Tel: (001) 800 462 3966
www.bedbathandbeyond.
com

Saks Fifth Avenue
Tel: (001) 877 551 7257
www.saksfifthavenue.com

S.D.H.
Tel: (001) 800 244 2688
www.sdhonline.com
(bedlinen)

**CURTAINS, TASSELS,
SOFT FURNISHINGS**

UK

Wendy Cushing
G7 Chelsea Harbour
Design Centre
London SW10 0XE
Tel: (01144) 020 7351 5796

Stuart Hands
Tel: (01144) 020 7373 0068

McKinney & Co
Studio P
The Old Imperial Laundry
71 Warriner Gardens
London SW11 4XW
Tel: (01144) 020 7627 5077
Fax: (01144) 020 7627 5088

FLOWERS

UK

Robbie Honey
Tel: (01144) 07932 697512

Annie Khan Florist
55 Hatton Garden
London EC1N 8HP
Tel: (01144) 020 7404 4048

Jane Packer
56 James Street
London W1M 5HS
Tel: (01144) 020 7935 2673
Fax: (01144) 020 7486 5097

Paula Pryke Flowers
20 Penton Street
London N1 9PS
Tel: (01144) 020 7837 7336
Fax: (01144) 020 7837 6766

Julie Roil
The Lanesborough Hotel
Hyde Park Corner
London SW1X 7TA
Tel: (01144) 020 7259 5599
Fax: (01144) 020 7259 5606

US

Bloom
541 Lexington Avenue
New York NY10022

Olivier Guigni at l'Olivier
Floral Atelier
19 East 76th Street
New York NY10021
Tel: (001) 212 774 7676
Fax: (001) 212 774 0058
Email: ognyc@aol.com
www.lolivier.com

FRANCE

Christian Tortu
6 Carrefour de l'Odeon
75006 Paris
Tel: 0033 1 43 26 02 56

FURNITURE

UK

Robert Grothier
602 King's Road
London SW6 2DX
Tel: (01144) 020 7736 6778
Fax: (01144) 020 7736 6360

Simon Horn
117–121 Wandsworth
Bridge Road
London SW6 2TP
Tel: (01144) 020 7731 1279
Fax: (01144) 020 7736 3522
www.shorn.com

Interiors Direct
The Studio
Lowdham Road
Gunthorpe
Nottingham NG14 7EQ
Tel: (01144) 0115 966 3111
Fax: (01144) 0115 966 4688
www.interiors-direct.net

Sasha Waddell
269 Wandsworth
Bridge Road
London SW6 7LT
Tel: (01144) 020 7736 0766
Fax: (01144) 020 7736 0746

Yeoward South
The Old Imperial Laundry
London SW11 4XW
Tel: (01144) 020 7736 4811
Fax: (01144) 020 7498 9611

US

Century Furniture
Tel: (001) 800 852 5552
www.centuryfurniture.com

Nancy Corzine
979 3rd Avenue #804
New York NY10021
Tel: (001) 212 758 4240
Fax: (001) 212 758 5644

Dakotah
www.dakotah.co.za
Email: josh@dakotah.co.za

Patina
Email:patinainc@
patinainc.com

South of Market
345 Peachtree Hills Avenue
NE ste 500
Atlanta
GA30305 ·
Tel: (001) 404 995 0802
(for Helen Ballard Weeks'
daisy table, see page 56)

BEDS

UK

Beaudesert
The Old Imperial Laundry
London SW11 4XW
Tel: (01144) 020 7720 4977
Fax: (01144) 020 7729 4970
www.beaudesert.co.uk

Judy Greenwood Antiques
657 Fulham Road
London SW6 5PY
Tel: (01144) 020 7736 6037
Fax: (01144) 020 7736 1941

US

Charles P. Rogers Beds
55 West 17th Street
New York NY10011-5513
Tel: (001) 800 727 7726
www.charlesprogers.com

UNUSUAL
FURNITURE

UK

Mark Brazier-Jones
Hyde Hall Barn
Buntingford
SG9 0RU
Tel: (01144) 01763 273599
Fax: (01144) 01763 273410
Email: studio@
brazier-jones.com
www.brazier-jones.co.uk

US

Keith Skeel at ABC Carpet and
Home, 4th Floor
888 Broadway
New York NY10003–1258
Tel: (001) 212 473 3000

Buzz Stone
2986 Nancy Creek Road
Atlanta, GA. 30327
Tel: (001) 404 351 5859
(wooden driftwood furniture)

DECORATIVE IRON-
WORK FURNITURE

UK

Louise Bradley
555 Kings' Road
London SW6 2EB
Tel: (01144) 020 7751 0081
Fax: (01144) 020 7751 0082
Email:
enquiries@louisebradley.
demon.co.uk

SCREENS

UK

Pukka Palace
Shrewsbury Road
Craven Arms
Shropshire
SY7 9NW
Tel: (01144) 01588 672846

US

Arte de Mexico
1000 Chestnut Street
Burbank
California
CA91506
Tel: (001) 818 753 4559
Fax: (001) 818 563 1015
Email:
artedemexico@aol.com
www.artedemexico.com

FIREPLACES

UK

Architectural Antiques
351 & 324 King Street
London W6 9NH
Tel: (01144) 020 8741 7883
Fax: (01144) 020 8741 1109

Ian Knapper
Tel: (01144) 01538 722733
www.ianknapper.com

Westland
St Michael's Church
Leonard Street
London EC2A 4ER
Tel: (01144) 020 7739 8094

Names in bold indicate people whose work is shown in this book. International dialling codes are shown in brackets.

Fax: 020 7729 3620
Email: westland@
westland.co.uk
www.westland.co.uk

US

Mackenzie & Dowd
2827 Northeast Martin
Luther King, Jr. Boulevard
Portland
OR 97212
Tel: (001) 503 282 4035
Fax: (001) 503 282 1559
Email: office@
mackenziedowd.com
www.mackenziedowd.com

Siteworks
Tel: (001) 800 599 5463
www.chateaustone.com

Stone Magic
Tel: (001) 800 597 3606
Email:
info@stonemagic.com
www.stonemagic.com

CARPETS

UK

Blenheim Carpets
41 Pimlico Road
London SW1W 8NE
Tel: (01144) 020 7476 2777
Fax: (01144) 020 7823 5210

US

ABC Carpet and Home
(see page 158)

Beauvais Carpets
201 East 57th Street
New York NY10022
Tel: (001) 212 688 2265
Fax: (001) 212 688 2384

PICTURES AND PHOTOGRAPHS

The Michael Hoppen
Gallery
3 Jubilee Place
London
SW3 3TD
Tel: (01144) 020 7352 3649
Fax: (01144) 020 7352 3669
www.gallery@
michaelhoppen-photo.com

The Stephanie Hoppen Gallery
17 Walton Street
London SW3 2HX
Tel: (01144) 020 7589 3678
Fax: (01144) 020 7584 3731
Email:
julia1@btinternet.com

ANTIQUES

UK

Alfie's Antique Market
13/25 Church Street
London NW8 8DT
Tel: (01144) 020 7723 5595

Kate Bannister Antiques
Angel Arcade
Camden Passage
London N1 8EU
Tel: (01144) 020 7704 6644

David Martin-Taylor
Antiques
558 Kings Road
London SW6 2DZ
Tel: (01144) 020 7731 4135

US

1st dibs
www.1stdibs.com
(online antique
shopping site)

GENERAL

UK

Design Museum
www.designmuseum.org

General Trading Company
2 Symons Street
London SW3 2TJ
Tel: (01144) 020 7730 0411
Fax: (01144) 020 7823 5426
www.general-trading.co.uk

Danielle Moudabber
Tel: (01144) 020 7225 1991
Fax: (01144) 0870 831 2413
(handbags and cushions)

Selfridges (see page 155)

Vo No Bi
35d Marylebone High Street
London W1U 4QV
Tel: (01144) 020 7224 2071

US

Robert Allen Home
Tel: (001) 800 240 8189 (US)
Tel: (001) 800 363 3020
(Canada)

The Designplace
The Home Depot
www.homedepot.com

INDEX

Figures in *italics* refer to captions